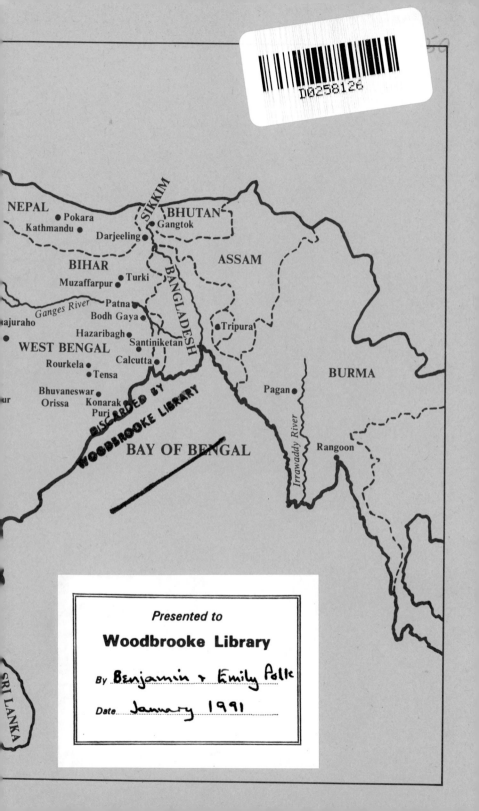

NEPAL
• Pokara
Kathmandu •
Darjeeling •

SIKKIM

BHUTAN
Gangtok

ASSAM

BIHAR
Muzaffarpur • • Turki

Ganges River
Patna •
Bodh Gaya •
Hazaribagh •

BANGLADESH

• Tripura

ajuraho

WEST BENGAL
Rourkela •
• Tensa

Santiniketan
Calcutta •

BURMA

Bhuvaneswar •
Orissa   Konarak •
Puri •

Pagan •

BAY OF BENGAL

Irrawaddy River

Rangoon •

SRI LANKA

D0258126

India
Notebook

India
Notebook

*Two Americans in the South Asia
of Nehru's Time*

BENJAMIN AND
EMILY POLK

Architect; poet and artist

*

MICHAEL RUSSELL

© Benjamin and Emily Polk 1985

First published in Great Britain 1985
by Michael Russell (Publishing) Ltd
The Chantry, Wilton, Salisbury, Wiltshire

Printed and bound in Great Britain

954

Contents

Note on the Illustrations

Apart from the temples, which somewhat predate us, the photographs at the end of this book illustrate our work and designs during those South Asia years.

B.P.

Foreword

Ben and Emily Polk are two remarkable Americans who travelled to India en route to their home in California and stayed twelve years, leaving their hearts there.

Attracted to the philosophy of Gandhi, they had met one of his followers in London in 1951 and accepted an invitation to see something of its practical expression in a village community in Bihar. This led to involvement in the building of a rural school, and the rest followed.

Ben is an architect, not then widely known in his own country, and not at all in the East. Yet he has left behind major buildings which have called forth the genuine appreciation of the people for whom they were built, no less than that of the architectural critics. For a foreigner with no previous experience of the East, no ready-made back-up organization, and working for the most part alone, to have designed and supervised the building of the National Memorial at Amritsar, a palace for the King of Nepal at Kathmandu and the great Buddhist Library in Rangoon, besides many other buildings in India, is an extraordinary achievement. That his work met with such approbation must surely be because both Ben and Emily studied deeply the religious and cultural background of the people for whom he was working. Absorbing this knowledge his buildings speak of what he calls 'the Spirit of the Place'.

Emily has an artist's observant eye and is able to transmit vivid and penetrating impressions, both in words and in drawings. Her warm outgoing friendship was extended to all those whom they met, whether Maharajas or 'sweepers'. So it causes only momentary surprise to learn that she was, at one time, President of the National Indian Association of Women, that august body founded by the British in the mid-nineteenth century.

To countries and peoples so different from their own Ben and Emily responded with love and understanding, and established a rapport which has eluded many Westerners with much longer experience. What they have to say, therefore, about Nehru's India is of more than passing interest.

September 1984   MARJORIE PASKIN

Authors' Note

In India ours were the Nehru years almost exactly. Peaceful, hopeful, idealist; or smug, somnolent, dogmatic – take your choice. For whatever is said of India will somewhere be true. Except for the Chinese invasion, and this was just a ripple, there were no crises. The hardships of the people were the grim, chronic ones of poverty, and yet their joy in life was richly evident. They were years which can never be repeated. Our experience there, perhaps like that of everyone in that amazing country, was in itself unique.

A few shining and faithful 'Europeans' (and this Indian term includes Americans) in the name of their religion and their love made the problems and the sufferings their own, and legions of unsung Indians did the same. We did not.

Notwithstanding, we did become a part of India. We lived its sweeter side, deeply mindful of the rest, but sure that if architectural work were to be done it quite simply would be through those with whom I could speak English and they, for the most part, were not in want.

My approach to architecture was welcomed in South Asia. Business-wise, I was under my own steam with no Foundation or government salaries, fellowships or grants. I was engrossed in my work the entire twelve years – and this accounts, though we were scarcely aware of it, for some of the odd omissions from our travel: no Kashmir, no Assam or Sri Lanka – there would always be time, we told ourselves, for the garden spots. And indeed a splendid eight months' study in the Kandyan Highlands came for us in 1980-81 and visits to India and Nepal also.

In this age, the world is building its intellectual structures within the spiritual frame (and the spiritual disarray) of the West. Whatever the splendors of the Eastern way, we did not doubt our

Western star, and we contributed something from that star to an India that gave so much to us. We found through England an India we loved for twelve years in the midstream of our lives, an India whose ways are nearly opposite to our American ways.

How did my wife and I come to India? There is no single answer. It was 1950. I took a diploma in regional planning in London; Emily found her lyric gifts in a poetry that 'suddenly appears, and, in the twinkling of an eye, is completed'; while both of us absorbed the sights and sounds and architecture of Europe.

The world is round. We were, in 1952, in Europe. So, home to California then, by way of India. And fate and fortune led us to find there another home.

Azeitão, Portugal BEN AND EMILY POLK
August 1984

I

In the Villages
1952

It was in Patna, on the Ganges, in Bihar 1952 in the hot month of May that we came to know in a few short days and nights the indelible force of the sights and sounds and smells that would always mean India.

The horse-drawn two-wheeled tonga from the station took us past parks and gardens where the fallen blossoms of flowering trees – orange-red gul mohurs, lavender jacarandas, and light-giving yellow cassia – made the air luminous over the red earth, and the 'rooms' between ground and branch glowed with these gorgeous colours. We breathed the hot smell of summer. Dust, and heat and scented flowers. Greens of winter were passing into dust. Crows, monkeys, orioles, cows, flowers, trees and people – people everywhere. We were caught in the kaleidoscope of India.

In London we had met Asha Devi. That was two years after Gandhi's death. Asha Devi and her husband, Aryanyakam, now guided Gandhi's Basic Education Center at Sevagram near Wardha in Central India. Asha Devi had said, 'Come.'

First, we had gone to Rasulia, the Friends' Center near the ancient town of Hoshangabad, in mid-India, a town of temples and huge trees on the banks of the sacred Narbadda river; then we went on to Asha Devi.

The welcomes were joyful ones that pointed to hopes for India and to their hopes for our part in village work. We heard and were shown in small schools and in the fields how Gandhi had worked for his belief that the villages were the key to India's future. We saw his small bare room, his sleeping mat, wooden shoes, and reading stand, a book notated in his hand. We heard and saw how deeply his presence had been felt, heard how the British had responded with understanding and how Gandhi and the British had over the decades mutually achieved independence for India in 1947, by and large through non-violent means; although the dreadfully bloody cost of Jinnah's Partition had not been reckoned with.

Hearing at first hand the magnitude of Gandhi's achievements, listening to details from those who had worked with him was a revelation, thrilling and compelling even in its aftermath – the stuff of the sagas of mankind.

For Mahatma Gandhi was a man of action. Immediately following Independence he had begun to establish his 'constructive program', the ramifications in daily living of his non-violent political technique. He envisaged a social order different from capitalist, socialist, or communist ones, an order based on love – decentralized, self-governing, and without exploitation. His name for this new order was 'sarvodaya', the rise of all.

We hoped to find fragments of this inspiration in the villages, for during the decades of his work it was to this eighty percent of India that Gandhi returned again and again in humility, to immerse himself and refresh himself in the timeless, rhythmic surge of village life. He longed to bring self-sufficiency and dignity to all his people, for relentlessly, through economic world-changes, the villages were suffering. He would restore them, not through large industry but by age-old small-scale means: his symbol, both political and economic, was the spinning wheel – everyone was equal in its use. He saw the truths of Hinduism, Islam and Christianity as timeless, and ready to be brought to reconciliation. In all these aspirations, the countryside was the focus for his work.

Within days of our introduction to the spartan life of Seva-gram, our opportunity came, and architecture was to be put to the test of service to village hopes. I was asked to go to the Rural University at the village of Turki, in north Bihar, near Muzaf-farpur, where new building was needed and to teach. Emily and I were delighted.

And so, Patna.

The Girls' School there was a two-storey building surrounded by trees. We were guests at the school and spread our bedding rolls on the tables of an upstairs classroom. The hot month of May is the wedding season in Patna. Non-stop loudspeakers blast away, full volume, their sentimental Indian film music day and

2

night. At 3 a.m. something resembling sleep had just come when a koel bird began to 'sing'. We had no warning. On a limb five feet from our beds, the deafening outburst began – a pump, a siren, and a scream! The effect was unnerving and sleep was banished for good.

I've never admitted that the bird's hysterical crescendo is a song, though Indian friends place it first for sweetness. In all our Indian years we had just three glimpses of this awful bird of night, a large species of cuckoo who, wisely, hides itself by day. But its 'song' is the soul of India, a magic cry of excitement and wonder which conjures up the rest.

The Girls' School – most students seemed to be from fairly well-to-do families – was a Gandhian school. Gandhi insisted on everyday demonstration of the dignity and worth of labor. Since the sweeper is almost at the bottom of India's social ladder, he chose this particular service as a routine for special emphasis, and the girls were at sweeper's work by 4 a.m. each morning, cleaning the school compound and the neighbouring streets. They sang at their sweeping, a lovely lilting bajan, a hymn, of Sita and Ram, who manifest the power of love in the Hindu pantheon.

We were introduced at an Assembly after classes at eleven that morning and said a few words. Occasions like this were a puzzle: how to meet the students' respect but still reach, on a common ground, ideas that could be of value to them? I had suspected from the start what soon became evident: in the countryside we would be learning far more than teaching.

There are fine museums in Patna, a city which in 330 B.C. was the capital of the great King Ashoka. We took rickshaws through the long sinuous spread of the city as it follows the river bank. We passed a parabolic dome of brick a hundred feet high built by the British in the last century for storing grain against famine. A spiral ramp led to the top and we could imagine the lines of grain-laden carriers, that once ascended the ramp to fill the vast space. We visited the site of Ashoka's wooden capital, where, miraculously, some of the post pilings of the palace are still preserved after two thousand years and, where excavated, the foundations can be clearly traced. And we went to Sarnath and the Deer Park where about 550 B.C. the Lord Buddha gained enlightenment. At Nalanda, the Buddhist University of 200 A.D., we saw the power of the ancient builders' artistry in brick.

But tomorrow we go to the village of Turki north of the river.

Sunrise on the Ganges at Patna in May merges the pale tints of sky and river. A heaviness of cool night air, silt-laden water, and sails of river boats – palest copper and tints of blue and pink. Some say the River Goddess, Ganga, could have leapt from the soul of the great Shiva as he sat in contemplation on Mount Kailash, in Tibet – Shiva, the transformer and the destroyer. But one need not put the river magic in Hindu terms. It is there for all. The ferry boat was lashed to the muddy shore – the bustle, the watching and waiting, the good offices to us who were without language, the courtesy of rural people, gave us the first sweet taste of India on our own. But we were squarely faced with that awkward question of language. Educated people even in the countryside frequently spoke English, but, usually Indian-English. The quick inflections of tongue and cadence, second nature in one's own tongue, are of course the last things acquired in a second language, and we found that on those occasions when we were invited to speak, much if not most was lost, and we were surprised to hear our brief comments spun out to great length. To teach or work effectively in the countryside we must surely learn Hindi. But in the event we learned perhaps a hundred words – no more.

Turki Village in the late afternoon – we were met by a delegation in a new bullock cart with rubber tyres! – we rode in style the mile and a half from the station at Turki to the Rural University. A mango and leechi grove of shading trees was centered on the reservoir-pond, about 300 feet square. Under the trees along two sides of the water stood the Rural University, temporarily sheltered in old but well-kept *katcha* houses of bamboo and mud, thatched with palm leaves. We learned to use the two words, *katcha* and *pukka*, the former meaning unfinished, unripe or of poor quality, and the latter ripe, or, permanent.

We were assigned what had been the University library, a *katcha* hut with walls of mud plaster four feet high neatly applied to a bamboo mesh framework left open above for light and air.

Across the pond from our house a small whitewashed temple shone with its own brightness in the green of late day. As the air cooled each evening before dark, fruit bats, the flying foxes, with three foot wingspread, swooped across the rosy sky above the water to the trees to begin their nightly feast. I hoped the new buildings I would begin would be as much a part of this lovely spot as this hut that was now our home.

I had seen the rapid weathering of the common sun-dried brick when left unprotected during the rains and I decided to conduct field experiments here with a rammed earth technique using admixtures to produce durability just as I had done in the United States in a small experimental house in Iowa.

Wherever seasonal farm work leaves time available to farmers, rammed earth has been, and still is, used in parts of Europe. But in assessing a rammed earth project for Turki, I realized that the Indian economy necessarily influences the whole range of design, and that construction processes would take advantage of abundant and cheap labor. In all of India expensive materials must be used with care, and the imported 'expert' must conserve them. At Turki, for instance, with rammed earth construction, the mechanical rammers I used in the United States, even if available in India, could not have been purchased.

The morning after we arrived, I was scheduled to give a lecture in the outdoor classroom under the trees. I said that tradition and custom represent the slowly accumulated wisdom that had developed the beauty we saw around us; that whatever changes we might attempt would be tested over the years and might be found wanting; that, as they themselves well knew, within the limits of the seasons' vagaries and the available tools, over the centuries villages have developed methods difficult to improve on. So, I said, we would see.

On our second evening Emily and I were honored guests at a 'cultural program' at a neighboring village. There is no gloaming in the tropics. The sun turns itself off at the close of day like an electric lamp; blackness is complete. We stumbled along in the dark on the earth dykes between the rice fields, with a hurricane lantern hissing up ahead.

Cultural programs as then provided by Government were village entertainment, laced with a measure of education, usually propaganda against the caste system – against those who preferred not to work with their hands – or (mildly) against purdah.

That evening the show was held in the open air around a square platform. Some 300 villagers sat on the ground, but we had a place of honor, exhibited toweringly on chairs placed beside the stage, just under the gasolene hurricane lantern. The chairs were more comfortable than the ground, if a bit over-conspicuous, but the bright hissing lantern was not. A whirlwind of insects gathered to sample the rare flavor of the foreign guests. The courtesy of being seated by the bright lights was one we never learned to appreciate, but we did learn to arrange our clothes to thwart most of the invaders. After our short speeches and the lengthy, mysterious translations, the show began.

In London we twice heard Indian music and liked it instantly. Here, on its home ground, we were again captivated when tabla, vocalist, sarod and tambura all went into action. Not a skilled performance to be sure, and the music subordinate to the performers who strutted and clowned. But here, in the country-side night air, ringed by hundreds of dimly-seen enthralled villagers, the excitement of the complex rhythms of the ragas had an elemental power and subtlety. There was plenty of energy as the players hurled themselves about in a folk drama. But for us the strong lead of the tabla was felt through it all, and it colors our memory of Turki. Music needs no interpreter.

Another invitation came before I could settle down to work. Elections were coming up and the Chief Minister of Bihar was in the area. Education officials had come to Turki from Patna, the capital, and with them I was to attend a Congress Party political rally in a small town some twenty miles away.

On a sweltering hot, pre-monsoon day, breathless, the white sun had torn all color from the landscape; glare from dusty fields erased all shadows. We went off in an open truck, seated on the deck behind the driver. A hundred feet down the rutted road the dust, pure white, high-quality flour-like dust, completely filled the air. Breath and vision were all but impossible for the next hour. But the elderly Patna leaders did not complain. This was their native land. They knew it well, their lives had been dedicated to it under the great Mahatma. The President of India, Dr

Rajendra Prasad, a colleague and disciple of Gandhi, was a native of Bihar. His home was nearby. Much violence had occurred here between Hindus and Muslims at the time of partition yet neither dust nor age could cloud the spirit of these veterans of those stirring, tragic years.

At the rally I was given a place of honor near the Chief Minister, a tribute to brotherhood across the sea. This was an occasion when lack of language was indeed a formidable barrier. No English was spoken; Bihar is the heart of the Hindi-speaking area of India. After the speeches, confusion, and music, we went outside the brightly colored tent. Village folk filed up to offer their respects to the Chief Minister and the most visible support came from local politicians with axes to grind.

On the way back through the dust toward Turki, we visited the home of a local landlord. A whitewashed brick house with tile roof, a central courtyard and reception rooms in front, separated from the women's domain behind. Servants plied us with tea and sweets and spiced *samosas*. We ate with our fingers and washed our hands both before and after tea. The Muslim custom of purdah still kept 'respectable' Hindu women completely out of sight.

Then, just arrived at Turki, a distant roar is heard. It multiplies itself through leaves and branches that are swaying wildly to its beat. The wind sweeps through, filling our little hut with dust, leaves, twigs. This unpleasant first blast blows on, and a clean cool wind rushes in, repairing the air. Now thunder is close overhead and the sky is continually alight with electricity. Flashes and sheets of lightning; an undulating curtain of brightness. Suddenly a sheet of rain approaches from across the fields, a remarkable rain, heavy and solid, each drop an enormous spoonful of water. The downrush lasted ten minutes? forty minutes? stilled itself, and began again.

When it finally ended the world was renewed, the air fresh and delicious. The wide mango leaves are polished to dark brilliant green, the pond has risen to cover the grass at its rim, fish leap joyfully in the quivering clear water. Children run out laughing, and bound splashing through just-formed pools shouting to one another. We shake out our limp belongings and enjoy a world awakened to the first of the monsoon.

Emily and I shared our hut with a mongoose who lived in the palm thatch overhead. Emily thought it was a special gift of the University, for mongooses wage perpetual warfare with cobras. When a cobra was killed inside the next door hut one night, with much bustle and shouting, we were even more pleased with our roommate. Next to us was a woodpile which was a haven for scorpions. Two woodcutters were bitten. We philosophized about a too obsessive carefulness – and the scorpions went their way and we went ours.

Kraits, however, are another matter. Five of my faculty colleagues and I, carrying our folded umbrellas, were strolling on the road in the cool of sunset, enjoying the first new greenery after that brief and early rain. All at once a band of small snakes appeared. They came toward us, not gliding, but jumping, in a kind of spring action – deadly poisonous and aggressive. Even cobras glide away, but kraits mean business. My colleagues, who, like most Indians, did not want to kill fellow creatures, flicked them away into the roadside ditch with their umbrella points in splendid unconcern.

There were cobras and scorpions, kraits and elephants, bats of all descriptions, water buffaloes and cows; and flies, flies, flies and mosquitoes by the millions. We took turns eating and fanning flies for each other, and we slept under heavy mosquito nets preferring to swelter than be hosts to hordes of starving mosquitoes. Emily, it seemed, had an iron constitution, but my scorn of special health measures went by the board after a ten days' bout with an 'unidentified fever'. After this I was as fussy as most other 'Europeans'.

The immediate purpose of my work was to construct two classroom buildings whose columns and foundations would be of burned *pukka* brick, but the walls of rammed earth. The longer range purpose was experimental: to see if rammed earth, more durable but also more expensive than sun-dried brick, would, on balance, with off-season farmers' labor, be economic throughout the area. These two objectives dovetailed nicely with Basic Education which is a village-level learn-by-doing program. It was also hoped that the University could thus escape the clutches of the Public Works Department, which I soon learned had a near stranglehold on public construction.

My building plan provided overhanging eaves and wide verandahs. Classrooms could be expanded by the seasonal shifting of the non-bearing walls of rammed earth block laid without mortar so that the verandahs could be included in classroom space during the rains. The blocks were large. The various earth mixtures rammed into place included a friable local lime rock, *kankar*, which underlay the soil of the area. It was mixed with coal tar, straw, powdered brick, lime, small percentages of cement, each block in different combinations and proportions. Such experiments by the students themselves, continuing over the years, would supply the need for buildings, and would comprise long range research of interest to the district as a whole.

I had expected the students would participate with me in the ramming process − hard work, in the hot months of May and June. But three laborers were hired instead, and I, the larger and the better fed, readily bore the brunt of the ramming.

I soon realized that certain axioms basic to an industrial economy were not basic to the countryside. For instance: time is money. Freshly burned lime for the mortar lay exposed, deteriorating while orders were not filled for the bricks. This would appear on the balance sheet.

What was really needed, and what I could not supply, was a preliminary educational process. Indians from the cities know the axioms of efficiency and could perhaps develop ways of teaching them in the countryside. Only after that, and as a second step, technical skills could be tested and would have meaning. I left Turki believing that the technological job in the villages was not the main one, except perhaps as a focus for the more important one of changing attitudes.

At all events, one memory was left with the villagers and students of Turki: a foreigner working hard with his hands in the hot sun of May and June, day after day. This must have seemed a sign of insanity, but even so, awe-inspiring.

I would guess that the building experiments were not completed. But the reader should not suppose this failure to carry out the work after I left stems from some inherent laziness of tropical peoples. I must emphasize that this is not so. Caste, false pride, and insufficient diet, my own failure to enlist support − perhaps the unsoundness of the idea itself for that matter – any or all of these would be an explanation. For I can say that I, in good health, have walked along the roads near Turki at noon in May with an umbrella and water, and quite literally have wondered whether I would make it, while on all sides were farmers working hard in the fields, men and women. There is no question of inherent laziness in India.

When our departure for Delhi was scheduled, a farewell banquet was given for us and for several of the faculty by the neighboring Hindu priest, the Mahant, who controlled much of the land and with whom my colleagues were not always in close agreement. But correct relationships between the University and his large establishment were maintained; he was a power in the area with great influence with the villages. He had, in fact, given land to the University.

The date of the feast and of our departure approached. The blue-black storm clouds of the full monsoon had piled up, the heat was wet and breathless. As we walked to our host's establishment, gusty signs of the full new season of rains could be plainly felt.

The Mahant was not a polished man. He spoke no English and made no effort to know or speak to us. But he had arranged a most delicious and elegantly served meal. We were all seated on the ground around two sides of the inner courtyard, a handsome space crowded with lush greenery. The Mahant took his place across the courtyard from us. Then young men in training with him, foreheads painted with the vermilion marks of Shiva, wrapped in fresh white cotton dhotis, placed before each of us a brilliant green banana leaf plate. Then a succession of puffed breads, rices, small servings of curried, pungent *dals* (lentils), fruits cooked in spiced sauces. Then bowls of fresh *dhai*, a clean-breaking yogurt, and the inevitable most excellent mango. The occasion was a high point for us, picturesque and delicious.

As we left the Mahant the rains came – all at once this time, decisively, and in buckets. The life of the year could begin again, the heat was broken, the crops would spring up. The voices of jubilant frogs pierced the roaring rain. We walked with our farewell escort along the ruts of the mud road two miles to the railway station. Emily lost a sandal in the mud; we were drenched and exhilarated.

More than once as the warm blinding deluge raged, we almost collided with water buffaloes, enormous, unwieldy black creatures moving like rudderless ships in a surging sea, symbolic and powerful.

Years later, at a client's request, I visited the ancient site of Vaisali where the Jain saint, Mahavira, had taught and disputed with Gautama, the Buddha, and had founded his own religion 2,500 years ago. Those ancient events are recorded in exhortations engraved in granite columns raised in 330 B.C. by Ashoka. One is near Turki. Passing Turki by train, I saw that the class rooms had been built as planned, but altogether of burned brick, and by the Public Works Department, after all.

'Gandhians' believed the greatest need after independence was for village leadership to emerge. Traditionally the capital seemed far away, a distant government, and local leadership was needed to develop cottage industries for villagers who did not customarily look to New Delhi for guidance.

Villagers blamed their ills on the party in power but Nehru was popular, personally. Communism found little response in the villages, although parts of North Bihar were later to become an outside-aided source of violent revolutionary movements. The feeling while we were there was that a religious-political reaction was the greater danger.

These were contributing reasons for my interest in the Sarvodaya approach which could perhaps cut through these conflicts, supplying the very urgent needs of village people for food, cloth, shelter and education. It would mean, for instance, the villagers would grow cooking oil seeds, process the oil and send the finished product to the towns – so reviving industry in the villages, which at present exported oil seeds for industrial processing, distribution, storage, and merchandising. The Sarvodaya people knew this re-ordering would take time, but wanted the purpose to be accepted as national policy. Rightly or wrongly, Nehru and the Congress Party could not bring themselves to abandon the established urban processing and marketing methods. It would be, they felt, a drastic disruption. Although Government had sponsored the Community Projects Program for village improvement, it forced expenditure schedules for 'successful' action which did not bring to the villages an understanding of community project principles.

In all this I believed I saw the political genius of Gandhi's spinning wheel symbol, and of his march to the sea to gather salt in defiance of the salt tax. This act was the Indian equivalent of our Boston Tea Party. And I believed I saw the wisdom of his insistence on local self-sufficiency in education.

There was, indeed, a learned man of God, doing great deeds in India then, Vinoba Bhave, a Hindu, a self-effacing but uncompromising man of action who had worked closely with Gandhi for many years. He was demonstrating the power of love to solve human conflict. His program was to secure voluntary gifts of land from the big landholders on behalf of the poor farmers. Vinoba had walked the length of India asking for gifts of land and there had been a strong, emotional response. He called together the annual Sarvodaya Conference of all Gandhian workers in India. In April 1954 they gathered under the mango trees at Bodh Gaya in Bihar, the place where the Buddha gained his enlightenment.

I was at the conference, walked and talked with our Hindu friends and I listened while Vinoba, sitting frail and white-robed said: 'People talk of the Russian revolution. America represents an example of a revolution of another type. But looking at both these countries I find that neither type is in accord with the genius of India. I firmly believe that India should be able to evolve, consistent with her ideals, a new type of revolution based purely on love. If people begin to donate their lands of their own free will, readily and generously, the whole atmosphere will undergo a change and India might well show the way to an era of freedom, love and happiness for the whole world. I hold to the belief that the moment we succeed in creating a society free from exploitation, the intellectual and spiritual talent of the people, which lies obscured at present, will shine forth. We, the believers of Sarvodaya, therefore have vowed that we will change the present structure of society. I have absolute belief in this mission, otherwise I could not have approached you to give away your lands so openly and unreservedly. I realize that God has rewarded my effort more than I deserve. I have no cause for complaint. All that I have to do is to explain the idea to the people.

'A psychological change like this cannot be brought about by war and violent revolution. It can only be brought about by the methods of Buddha, Christ, Ramanuja and other great teachers. Ultimately it is to be the dedication of one's all for the well-being of all. Unless the existing social order which is based on inequality, strife, and conflict is replaced by one founded on equality and mutual cooperation, there can be no salvation for mankind.'

To meet with Vinoba was to find an evenness of world vision and a careful weighing of action in terms of religious purpose. And these were the qualities he sought to inculcate in his own helpers by setting an example through action. Our business, he taught, is with the deed and not with the result. Inactive meditation is not the right course; but action should be without attachment and without desires.

How, I wondered, would Vinoba's teachings tackle such problems as the limiting of population, increasing agricultural production, expanding education? Here, I found, was a group, who believed that *how* we produce the necessities of life, *how* we organize our politics, *how* we educate our children – that all these methods define the quality of our approach to God and the quality of our strength in non-violence. Added to its history of philosophical idealism, India was now a nation where members of Government had behind them the facts of non-violent power as demonstrated by Gandhi, as well as the Congress Party's stabilizing principles.

It was not surprising, therefore, to find at the Bodh Gaya Conference, Prime Minister Nehru, the President Dr Rajendra Prasad, Vice-President Radhakrishnan and the Congress Party Secretary as well as Cabinet Ministers who had come at Vinoba's invitation. As I watched these men of world thought seated on the ground under the trees, the movement for land gifts seemed to have about it that important quality of world movements – the ability to attract leaders, and the ability to focus allied methods of thought and action on a diversity of problems.

However, it was apparent that if Vinoba's way was to be demonstrated it would be in personal relationships within small groups. Only that could be the setting for social and individual evolution. I questioned the Sarvodaya leaders about Nehru's goal of state socialism – could it be reconciled with Sarvodaya? The reply was that production must be reorganized on a small scale basis, that bureaucracy must be eliminated. The Sarvodaya thinkers had not yet come to grips with the large city. So I began to wonder if the time had passed when Gandhi's dream for India might be feasible. To be sure, land gifts were made to Vinoba, there was progress in education and agriculture, but the age-old questions of how shall local and national economics be reconciled were not sufficiently well answered.

Gandhi's dream is the eternal dream of mankind. He is rooted in history. In one way or another I was convinced that a more prosperous countryside remained the key to India's future, but not just for the sake of the rural areas themselves. The solution of the ills of India's large cities, too, lies in the prosperity of its villages. It was to the city, inevitably, that Emily and I returned. For an architect it must be so.

Thirty-one years later, in 1983, B. L. C. Johnson in his *Development in South Asia* could write:

'Indian politicians and planners have been vehement in insisting on the need for equity, but they seem unable to resolve the contrasting viewpoints of the founding philosophers of independent India: Nehru with his belief that Government knows best and so should exert tight and direct control from the top; and Mahatma Gandhi with his romantic ideal of the peasant as the starting point for national development.'

Even in the Five-Year Plans conflicts were spelled out. This, from the Third Plan: 'In the short run there may sometimes be a conflict between the economic and the social objectives of developmental planning. The claims of economic and social equality and those of increased employment may have to be reconciled with the requirements of production,' in other words, with the accumulation of capital.

Today at Rasulia, guided by Marjorie Sykes, an English Quaker who has made Indians and India her life and home, practical details of self-sufficient agriculture and village industry are being demonstrated. Mahatma Gandhi would be proud of this.

In the other direction was to be the 'green revolution' achieved in the '60s and '70s throughout much of India and Pakistan with fertilizers and pesticides. India needs both approaches – and indeed, all approaches. In Pakistan and north India irrigation farming, capitalist in essence, and based on the great works left by the British, is now bringing relative prosperity to the countryside.

2

Karachi, Rangoon, Amritsar
1952 – 1954

The Government of Pakistan commissioned me to design the Polytechnic Institute in Karachi – but without provision for the architect's supervision of construction. This is the way of Public Works Departments the world over. I had already an office in New Delhi, and now in 1953 it was necessary to establish an additional office in Karachi. I brought in English and American draftsmen to assist with working drawings since in Pakistan there were no men trained for large work.

The site was necessarily in the desert among knife-sharp rocks in the white heat. There would be a strong design, as with the old desert builders who created the courtyard oasis behind wind-protecting walls. Machine layouts in the workshops for the twelve trades had two needs in common: good ventilation, and ample daylighting without direct sun. In Karachi sky-brightness is roughly twice that of comparable days in temperate zones. Electricity was too scarce a product to waste in daytime lighting of windowless buildings. Distribution of sunlight evenly, but not directly, in the rooms was the goal. The 'butterfly' monitor roof I had developed in the forties for residential construction in California was used again for light control in this totally different world, light being made to reflect from walls. Shock-concrete adjustable louvers gave flexibility, ventilation and security.

Emily and I wrote about these things at the time: 'From earliest days basic architectural opportunities remain much the same, but today's architecture more than any other must be a "thinking" architecture. Our time has lost most of the instinctive rationale that guided the ancient builders in their unerring creation of works of art. Our challenge is greater but, established on the past, we may apply new techniques as tangible milestones for the future.'

The designs and working drawing were completed and then I was down with jaundice. Our friends at Karachi's Indian High Commission came to the rescue. In New Delhi they had once before prescribed miscellaneous and successful homeopathic remedies. Now came the prescription for jaundice: the juice of raw sugar cane. It worked, but it took time – while the peculiar depression of this illness, deepened by the nightly barking of the street dogs, the constant bluster of wind and blowing sands, spoiled whatever chance I might have had of loving Karachi.

For air travel those were the terrible months of high winds, dust and sand storms that blank out all vision with a thick red veil for thousands of feet in the air. The plane flights to and from Delhi were unnerving. In Karachi there was only sand, and sun – too much sun – and camels and refugees and flies. Karachi was an unlovely place.

There was an immense difference between the two countries – India and Pakistan – and the two peoples. The obvious ones were, of course, purdah, and the austere Islamic mode of worship without ikons, single-minded. And India the reverse and with its vast complexities. Americans and most Europeans, could more easily accept the direct Islamic attitudes, but not the Hindu's. Pakistan was strongly pro-American, India was not. Pakistanis and Americans enjoyed each other. There was mixing at cocktail parties (not so in India, then) and an upper-class sympathique on both sides.

But there were flaws behind this silver sheen: at the top level of Government I met few Pakistanis who seemed to care what happened to their nation. They had been handed a country to run with no preparation for political life. Those Pakistanis with whom I dealt directly, those in the middle ranks of the hierarchy, were as distressed as I. These men had been the first to envisage the Polytechnic project, and had developed educational programs for it. Their hearts were in its future. Eventually they found themselves out of Government altogether, their concern and their efficient work unappreciated.

But in the course of all this agony, over work and distress there were refreshing interludes at the sea. There is a keyhole rock at Belagi, twenty-five miles west on the coast of Baluchistan where English friends had a cottage for a week of seclusion and change of pace. And there was the beautiful ancient group of Persian mosques at nearby Tatta.

Soon I was commissioned by the Government to design the Karachi College of Domestic Science for Women – a new step for the Muslim world. This was in 1952. It, like the Polytechnic, was Ford Foundation sponsored. Functionally the college was of value, but the Works Department built it with a heavy hand: the feminine delicacy of the design was lost. It was my first and last collaboration with a Public Works Department.

Karachi, on balance, was my trial by fire. From its terrors came a further commission, also Ford Foundation sponsored – the Tripitaka Library in Rangoon, a Buddhist research library housing modern techniques of library management. I was invited by the Prime Minister of Burma, U Nu, to go to Pagan, the ancient capital, on the Irrawaddy River in the north to search out the historic roots of Burmese architecture.

Before I left, the Prime Minister told me tales of two architects of ancient times. The first built so magnificent a pagoda for his client, the King, that to avoid the risk of even finer works for other princes, the architect was decapitated. The second architect, when his pagoda was completed and the King found it possible to insert a pin in one of the mortar joints met the same fate. The Prime Minister beamed.

The trip to Pagan was by single-motor plane as far as Chowk on the Irrawaddy, then by river boat, and finally by jeep to a guest house built in the 1920s for, but never occupied by, the Prince of Wales. The surrounding country was in the hands of the rebels and I was thoughtfully provided with a squad of soldiers as protection against kidnapping. But as we disembarked from the river boat at the jungle's edge at night in the blinding glare of searchlights, it was clear enough that there would have been an easier way than kidnapping for the rebels to terminate our operations.

The classical age of architecture ended in Pagan in the thirteenth century with the ruthless invasions of Ghengis Khan, leaving a magnificent city of large pagodas completely deserted. Generally pyramidal in silhouette, expertly built of brick with stucco ornament, the city has remained virtually intact in the surprisingly dry climate of middle Burma. The vibrant equipoise between the horizontal and the vertical which is so overwhelming with the Indian Hindu temples of the eleventh and twelfth century, is softened in these Buddhist pagodas of Greater India to a mighty serenity, paving the way for later influences from China that also became part of Burma's heritage.

Back in Rangoon a number of highly symbolic elements had revealed themselves to the Prime Minister as necessary to the design of the building – eight entrances (The Eightfold Noble Path of Buddhism), three floors (The Three Baskets of Wisdom, or Tripitaka), a circular plan, twenty-four windows, one hundred and eight lotuses – these were to be made a vital part of the building, the core of its spiritual function. It behoved the architect, therefore, to try to comprehend the serenity of the Buddha, to evolve once more a contemporary expression of age-old truths – truths to which the Sixth Buddhist Council, convened in Rangoon for 1955, would be addressing itself. The building was to last for 2,500 years, the end of the next Buddhist epoch. I could not guarantee it!

In Pagan I saw the traditional Burmese pointed arch indigenously developed without European contact and flowing from the same law of gravity and structural need as the romanesque of France and England. The stone quarries of North Burma were in the hands of the rebels. Advanced concrete techniques were out of the question in Burma at that time, so the use of mass reinforced concrete was the only workable answer to the problem of materials. But, and this was of more importance, the spirit of Burma could be well interpreted in this massive medium. This arch would now be made to partake of the nature of reinforced concrete with its capacity to resist tension in bending. The inner arches of the Library would be curved in plan and bound in to the central core of the building as stamen and pistil forms at the center of a flower.

Three building-wings were placed about the central circular core – on either side a public library and an auditorium, and opposite the entrance, a religious museum. The central core itself was reserved for scholars and monks of the Institute of Advanced Buddhist Studies – a sanctuary for research and meditation.

The plays of interior light and shade would be reminiscent of Pagan's Ananda Pagoda where shafts of light, arranged from above, indirectly illumine the giant gilded figures of four Bodhisatvas – those enlightened men who are at the threshold of Nirvana.

Here, clerestories at three levels would light the circulation space surrounding a court that would reach up from the ground to the pinnacle of the building. Rigorous arch forms of white concrete would sing against the richly colored moldings of the background walls, while accents of the strongly modelled fountain and the iron railings would be picked out in the semi-precious stones of north Burma. The gilded chandeliers of the central core could provide additional spatial play. The radial manuscript-book stacks would surround these large spaces.

Ancient palm leaf documents in the Pali script transmitting teachings central to Buddhism were salvaged after most were destroyed by the Japanese in World War II. Laboriously collected replacements were gathered from the few monasteries of the countryside that had not been overwhelmed in the last days of the South-East Asia war. This perishable treasure would be the nucleus of the Library.

In none of this, nor in my other traditional Asian work, was there any copied duplication. One studies the past intently and then, before design begins, one dismisses it from the conscious mind. A residue remains, and this is continuity. But it is always fresh. This, properly, is what is meant by aesthetic 'conservatism'. And in this proper sense the conservative may be the true radical.

The very ancient Buddhist Great Stupa at Sanchi in India, with its enclosing circular railing and outlying gateways is an unequalled expression of the Buddha's eternal peace. As one moves on the circular path between the Stupa and the railing, the sequence of perspectives revealed at intervals between the gateways is anchored always to the vast circle of the stupa which remains ever the same. In Rangoon, the enclosing garden walls circling the Library building would provide such an experience. Within the wall would be bronzes, pools, and luxuriant planting, the wall's outer face being deeply wrought with integral concrete patterns derived from Pagan. The mass of the building would sail firmly on the mass of the land. There would be still a further circle of sacred blossoming trees, and beneath one of these, in 2,500 years, the next Buddha would be born.

The spell of buildings should not end with their walls but should be a part of earth and air and sky, making these, if the building is worthy, more beautiful than before the building came, and drawing in return from the power of the land. When this is so, the *genius loci* speaks.

Nature is bountiful in Burma. Across the wide Irrawaddy at Pagan, a line of emerald hills, their summits dotted with dazzling white pagodas, is matched with other hills behind the ancient city. The pagodas are now interspersed with pleasant villages where older craftsmen teach the art of lacquer work.

The villagers may sense the harmonious symbolism about them without need for word or diagram.

But for a scholarly Buddhist like U Nu, words, thoughts, buildings, the senses themselves were all symbols leading to high knowledge. U Nu was a fine person, a deeply religious Buddhist. It was my job to understand and express his purposes in architectural form. Analogies should not be pressed too far, but whether the building be the heart of a flower with its pistil (the fountain) in the green forest with the blue sky and the gilded sun above; or whether the metaphysics of Buddhism be literally demonstrated in symbolic numbers, the essential goal of the Tripitaka Library can be taken to be that 'matter, weight, and mass become a living reality and a latent energy, a magic substance full of hidden activity', as Anagarika B. Govinda has put it in his study of Stupa Symbolism. In the Buddhist sense, there is no essential difference between matter and mind or between the outer and the inner world. In Buddhism the objective *becomes* the subjective. In Asia, through age-old symbolisms, architectural expressions of metaphysics seem almost instinctive. Such forms as square and cube reveal order; the circle is the form of life and energy: pyramidal shapes were steps in the ascent of man towards God. Then there are in Buddhism psychological statements of the connections between form-color-sensation and the states of consciousness and meditation. There is a fusion of architectural elements growing from the earth itself, the structure on which the Buddhist builds his life.

The numbers four and eight are characteristic of the ground plans of ancient religious monuments. There are to be studied the horizontal elements, the four foundations of mindfulness, the four great efforts, the four fundamental meditations. Then in the vertical direction the number three is evidenced: the three principles of life, the three principles of action, the three principles of existence – these being the universal aspects of metaphysics. Verticality was developed in symbolism all the way up to the umbrellas, or cones, which topped the ancient stupas.

The Buddhist who is willing to see the Hindu concepts within which Buddhism, in fact, arose, would agree with the unity of the two guiding Hindu principles: the principle of Shiva, the transformer, and the principle of Vishnu, the law; sometimes paraphrased as Shiva the destroyer, and Vishnu the preserver. The plant cannot be born before the seed has perished. Freedom and the law become One – almost. A third Hindu principle, Brahman, or birth and materialization, is the overlapping residue in Hinduism to which Buddhist philosophy addresses itself. The Buddhist aim is to free oneself from this constant 'becoming' through understanding of, and action according to, the laws of enlightenment. The intricate intertwining of Hindu and Buddhist architectural forms all the way from the hemispherical stupa at Sanchi in mid-India through the vertical *sikhara*-like form of the temple at Bodh-Gaya in Bihar, built on the spot where the Buddha attained enlightenment, and on across south Asia to the Pagodas of middle Burma at Pagan and beyond are not mere borrowings and improvisations but represent the formal development of these principles. I hope the Tripitaka Library in some way in the twentieth century also measured up to this high purpose.

There were lighter moments, or at least more personal ones. Coming from the unwarranted Government pomp of Karachi I was welcomed, on first meeting, at the site-to-be, on a rainy day by the Honorable Prime Minister of Burma, who drove up in a jeep, dressed in sandals and short sleeves. He held an umbrella over us as we walked.

And then there was the formal dinner, marking the signing of my design contract, at which I was presented, lo and behold, with a blueprint which was to be the 'design' of the building. The dinner was less than a success when, as I thought of George Washington, I could not lie politely about the horrors of this drawing. Matters were patched up, however, and I went my own way design-wise, having understood that the intention of the sketch was to indicate symbols only.

The building was constructed 'departmentally' by direct Government action, but this time with the supervision and control of the architect. We found an excellent site engineer in India, Visvanath Jhanjee who loyally and ably stayed by the work of construction through five difficult years of political vicissitudes as U Nu and General Ne Win alternated in power. And then the happy ending with the building complete and a splendid dedication ceremony personally planned by U Nu – special prayers, eighty gongs and specially struck gold medals for Jhanjee and for me – I am Maha Theippa Guru, a 'great master of science and arts'. And the Prime Minister himself graciously served to Emily and to me the first two dishes of the succeeding banquet.

And finally an anonymous issue of a colored calendar of the Tripitaka Library, well photographed, somewhat garish, all in Burmese with cigarette ads across the bottom. The building had entered folklore – although at present it is still for scholars only.

Now twenty-five years later, I wonder what will be the fate of this building, built 'to last 2,500 years', where simple people throw themselves down in reverence at the very spot where my Chinese carpenter foreman had been murdered it was said by the rebels, and where I removed from Burma my first site engineer, found drinking on the job. Will its day of veneration be short-lived? Politics, perhaps, will tell.

During the '50s the atmosphere of Burma was as different from that of India as an April shower from a strong monsoon. With no caste system, Burma had a light touch, was ever unpredictable. India suffered from too much bureaucracy, Burma from a lack of it. No population problem, no food shortage in Burma. But there were arms left over from World War II, freely used by the countryside rebels. And there was political unrest because of proximity to China.

New design work was coming along.

Deserting the New Delhi drafting room for the countryside and places of old temples in order to find a change of pace and a recollection, as I often did, Emily and I went to the south by train and country bus seeing much of ancient India on our way.

First, Khajuraho in the Vindya Hills near Chhatarpur with its magnificent temples, especially to the Kandariya Mahadeo temple which seems literally to force itself upward from the center of the earth. Since this is, without question, India's strongest architectural work – even considering the Taj Mahal – we must pause to consider it. The symmetry of the temple is fundamental and organic. It is not perceived as façade architecture but as the impact of volumes experienced in space. The Hindu form of worship includes a walking around the object of veneration: the temple itself was such an object.

Older organic shapes can be perceived in the final stone: the curve of bamboo prototypes or the stacking of logs to form the spire, *sikhara*, the temple's most striking feature. Organic growth is again inferred by the ornament that grows from points where one form type changes to another, as leaflets at the point where branches emerge from a stem.

The temple forms follow the dictates of the law of gravity which good architecture always follows. The convex curve of the temple spire, the *sikhara*, approaches the parabolic curve in which the weight of masonry is perfectly at rest, in which there is no element of bending, so that the structure is in direct compression – the most stable of masonry stresses.

Here it is the quickening of tempo in the tension and release of upward rhythm, and a complexity of the interlocked horizontal and vertical rhythms, which concentrates the power of mountains into a work of man. This slightly convex sikhara silhouette and the opposite concave shapes of the enormous temple gates of Madurai in South India offer the dynamic way of building vertically. Esthetically, it is the most vigorous way of transferring man's energy to a landscape form. The strong light of India requires deep modulation of these basic forms, so sculpture was a part of architecture. This was the mode of architectural thought that swept over all South Asia in the bygone centuries of expanding Indian culture.

Hindu and Jain temple architecture is symbolic, monumental.

The ancient Indian texts on architecture, the Vastuvidya, dwell on these semi-religious theories. The temple was the likeness of the universe and also analogous to the human form. Proportions were laid down and sometimes based, as with Vitruvius, on the size of a man with arms extended – and yet in the outcome, intuitive leadings free from rules finally governed the design. The Hindu skill with numbers brought out the idea of the 'remainder' which gives birth to new life, an idea gained from the fact that the immutable cycles of astronomy, the month and year, for example, are incommensurate. But even with all the magical concerns and notwithstanding the very conservative purpose of temple architecture there was still no mechanistic uniformity.

The Vastuvidya also describes in detail the processes of site selection. The temple should be near water where the gods are at play in eternal creative joy. The site must be purified and dedicated. The architect's year-long ceremony of ploughing would have thoroughly familiarized him with the spirit of the place, its shape, geology, and esthetic connotations before he began work on the design. Reverence for life's order was a part of these rites. The ultimate development of Hindu thought asserts there is but one cosmic mind, one God, and harmony with him was the purpose of the architect's work.

In 1919 a day of terror had come to Amritsar in the Punjab. And the tragic events there in the open space that is the Jallianwalabagh, that searing day in 1919 was the harbinger of the loosing of India's bond to Britain.

The British, alarmed at the growing restlessness of an India which after 1,000 years of foreign rule was awakened by Mahatma Gandhi to the possibility of 'self-rule, within the Empire if possible, without, if necessary', had passed a number of coercive measures. There were mass meetings and demonstrations all over India. The British countered with a ban on all meetings of citizens.

But the men of Amritsar gathered quietly in the heat of the day under the trees of the Jallianwalabagh to plan a protest. The British blocked the two gates, manned the roofs of surrounding buildings and fired on the unarmed gathering. Through this event the nation's determination was forged – the British must go.

Forty-two years after, in 1961, the Jallianwalabagh was again thronged with people. Men and women from all parts of India, the President of India, the Prime Minister, many of the greatest of the nation's leaders, her thinkers, and holy men gathered in a gentle pre-monsoon rain to dedicate the first national memorial of independent India.

Emily and I strolled through the garden under our umbrella. We stood quietly rejoicing in the delight of those who looked into the great reflecting pool, those who admired the enormous sandstone lanterns.

I had been introduced to the Jallianwalabagh National Memorial Committee, headed by Mr Nehru, by Rajkumari Amrit Kaur, Minister of Health in Mr Nehru's cabinet, a former princess of Christian Sikh heritage, a charming gentlewoman who had devoted her life to the service of India and who had walked with Mahatma Gandhi.

An architectural design can be a policy instrument, and this one proved to be so; for my first design caught the imagination of the Prime Minister and there was never a hitch from that point on. The project was close to India's deepest feelings and aspirations, her first national memorial. It was necessary to see oneself as wholly Indian.

I travelled to the Jain Temple cities of the extreme west, Girnar and Politana. Built in the days of the Muslim invasions, the precious temples – placed high on mountains behind austere stone fortifications – were forests of delicate *sikhara*, spires crowding the levels of stone, and juxtaposed sharply against the strong defense works.

The weather was superb, and on the long day's walk there were lakes for swimming. This was the lion country of India – though I saw no lions – and on every side, a thing not common in our world, beauty from the past was well lived-in today. Here, in these ancient empty cities was the thrilling simultaneity of horizontal and vertical vibration of the temple form. It seemed clear that this was a formal unifying mode for most of India, and now the spinning wheel of Gandhi, another potent sign of national purpose, would be added to it.

Back in New Delhi I detailed each stone of the relief pattern. It

26

was satisfying to work with some of the finest stones in the world, the native red and white sandstone of Dholpur, and the red granites of Mysore. Although the craft of masonry work has been lost, as in most places the world around, there are many in India who still skillfully hold the chisel and beautifully copy the templates of design. But it was necessary to supply the craft-knowledge myself, and to see it faithfully carried out at site.

The work is in solid red sandstone ashlar – none of the thin veneers that characterize both Muslim and modern Indian work (except for the fine exception of Lutyens's Viceroy's Palace in New Delhi which is indeed of solid stone). The memorial is built to last the centuries, a forty-five-foot high *sikhara* form, framing the relief pattern of a flame of martyrdom. It rises from a reflection pool and is flanked at the corners by huge sandstone lanterns capped horizontally with white stone slabs, all molded in the Indian fashion. The slabs are poised as if in vibrancy they had forced themselves from the depths of the waters, still holding their white stone tablets high to mark their reverence. The form of the flame, the central monument itself, is dominant, like the *sikhara* of the temple. At the four corners of its base is the *chakra* in red granite, the symbol of dynamic peace, Ashoka's wheel of life, Gandhi's spinning wheel. This monument beckons to brotherhood, and there is no echo of bitterness; Indian forms are given a new meaning.

It was to have stood within an enclosure of cypress trees as a quiet sanctuary, but over the years the trees were not attempted. An ancient tomb already exists here, and that, together with an historic well, gives contrast of incident to the formal design. From across the wide lawns of the garden the flame, the stone lanterns, and the nearby fountains are seen with the reflection pool as one enters the Bagh, the six-acre garden, through the low-lying sandstone pavilion which completes a place of refuge and of reverence.

On the basis of my meetings with Mr Nehru while working on the Memorial, I would like to put down here some of my thoughts and observations concerning him and concerning Gandhi.

I met Mr Nehru alone and at Committee meetings and at the Bagh on four or five occasions, so my personal impressions of him are very limited. He was deeply interested in the Memorial design and after the first showing knew well the details. He was obviously a thoroughly fine man of keen intelligence. He was impatient when his colleagues were not up to the mark. There was a marked deference to him which was understandable; but often that deference was exaggerated in his presence by those who were unsure of themselves. It was an exaggeration of a wonderful Indian courtesy, which however, when in the shadow of a man of special eminence became an excuse for doing nothing – for letting him take the lead in everything, and coasting on his initiatives. This paralysis in his presence naturally hindered the functioning of his government, and it could also have emphasized, or perhaps developed latent personality traits, that even the best of men, too long in absolute power, must face.

Mr Nehru claimed no such stature as Gandhi's. Educated in the British school, he saw the weakness of the Indian way as the possibility of a failure to act. It was the frequent lack of action in getting on with the job that visibly annoyed Mr Nehru. There is a delightful self-revealing book of fables from India's ancient past, the Panchtantra (which antedates our Aesop's fables by several centuries), that affords secret amusement to a Westerner as he catches the flavor of Indian ways. The keen wit of the book is satire at its best and one could imagine Mr Nehru smiling somewhat wryly over these ancient stories still today so apt.

But in assessing Nehru as an Indian leader he must be seen juxtaposed with Gandhi. And in those first years of Independence in the background of everyone's thought was reverence for the memory of the Mahatma, and an ever-present challenge to meet in his spirit the myriad new problems of Independence. So what of Gandhi? In what lay the greatness of this man? I think it lay in the fact that he was a politician who gained just and right purposes through what has been called non-violence, but what can better be called the power of Truth. There is much misunderstanding of Gandhi, especially in India itself. It is far more comfortable for us lesser spirits to equate his role to sainthood: since we are by no means saints, how can we expect ourselves to follow him or to try what he tried?

Gandhi was transparently a religious man – but there are many religious men. His greatness was not in this. His greatness for the world was as a practicing politician who tried to let the power of

God, of Truth, come into politics where before the stream of violence had run. And this was true in both national and international affairs insofar as they came into his fields of action; though I believe his refusal to assist Britain during World War II was thoroughly unwise.

In future times Gandhi will be seen either as an isolated mountain top of human potential, or, if we manage it, as the beginning of a new era.

For India herself, his greatness was broader than this. He gave Indians personal courage after the centuries of Muslim and British domination. His many-sided activities in education, social reform, village economics, and politics suited the genius of his people and spoke to them in their own terms. When he said that truth and love were to become the means for the regeneration of their lives, it rang true and they responded, no matter what their walk of life, caste, or economic status. And it may be that this high moral level in the world of action and achievement will yet be recognized by westerners – whose problems today are the reverse of India's. His way is a guide to that re-establishment of value and of purpose without which we will fail in small issues as well as large.

If there was a spiritual heir to Gandhi it was Vinoba – not Nehru. But neither Vinoba, nor probably Gandhi himself, could have done the work a day job a Prime Minister is called to do.

A long perspective is called for when looking back on the British Raj. There is no evidence that an ideal pre-British state of affairs existed in India which was wantonly destroyed. The British were heirs to an anarchical situation in the countryside. The 800 years of Moghul rule had been stable on balance, but during its decline after Emperor Aurangzeb died in 1707, local governors and robber chiefs raised private armies and warred for territory. British rule put an end to their cruel oppression of the villagers. Above all else the British administration wished to be fair, consistent, reasonable and efficient. And it was.

3
Letters and Notes

Dearest Lili,

I've been here, with Irene and Vivian Bose for two weeks. Ben is in Karachi. Exciting things in architecture have developed for him. We've travelled so much that it's heavenly to be still for a while. I love it here with Irene, can breathe deeply, look around myself, sit in the sun, smell flowers. Vivian is always hard at work as one of India's Supreme Court justices.

What do I do otherwise? Well, the other day I looked for poetry in Irene's wide garden. Sat down on a patterned chair. 'If poetry is here, and I'm quiet, it will come out onto the grass and cavort as poetry should, trailing slight mists through tree shadows, darting under thorn thickets and out again. Perhaps it will climb that flowering tree and swoop down disguised as a bird to drink at the pool.'

I sat still a long time. A large brown and yellow wasp, carrying a bit of mud to add to his igloo, swerved past me. Yellow Sulphur butterflies eddied together in a fluttering ecstatic gossip, eddied in and out of the tall-cascaded yellow flowered acacia tree, and breezed apart to dance quivering on the air with other random partners, then with others still.

Then at the far end of the garden a mongoose came from the shadow with an uncertain run. Its silver fur shimmered like treasure as the sun caught the undulant movements. It disappeared under a thorn thicket. Was it hunting for cobra?

He came out again, rippled in the shadows, long fluffed tail curving through the grass. He moved quickly on delicate feet, a few steps one way then the other. Those nimble feet are the defense it uses against the cobra. He is like a small quadruped St

George forever defeating dragons; apparently neither for food or malice, but with dispassionate purpose, a sense of social duty enlisted against an evil. Not waiting for the evil to happen, the mongoose goes calmly in search of it. They say he allows the snake to strike, leaping quickly onto its outthrust head, to dance with agile virtue until the neck of the evil is broken. Shaking its silken armour into place, the mongoose continues his mission.

The little saint at the end of the garden rippled around trees, under shrubs, looking for frogs, scorpions, rats or young birds for dinner. His crusading spirit is tainted with a passion for the flesh of fowl; a well-stocked hen house is his deluxe restaurant.

A tree-pie swooped with a bounce onto the water pipe, jerked his long tail experimentally, hopped to the ground to drink escaping water, ignoring the ornamental pool a wing-spread away. A troup of babblers scurried hysterically across the terrace near me. A feather floated down and settled on a stone. I stood up and stretched, and made a mental note 'some poetry, some prose . . . '

Marina Hotel, New Delhi
Dec. 29, 52

Dearest Mother,

Irene and Vivian have gone to their home in Nagpur so I'm back at the hotel. Delhi is *cold*! Our heavy clothes are at rest in trunks at Ben's mother's in Des Moines! Like California, houses and buildings are not made for cold weather. Rooms can be simply bitter. Imagine, in India, wearing a woolen shirt, two sweaters, a jacket and being chilly!

Ben was here from Karachi during Christmas week. He'll be there for another two months. I want very much to go there and be with him.

We're again in the two pleasant rooms at the Marina. I've become quite fond of this unfashionable old hotel. It's built like a ship, with long curving decks, and it's just in the middle of New Delhi.

Going down to dinner these cold nights, walking along the open-to-the-sky verandahs wrapped up warmly, I look down over the balustrade into cold blue night mists that have turned the street lights below to a strange luminous violet. Everything dark

31

and glowing. People, horsecarts, autos, bicycles, push-carts, go by below in the dark like blue shadows. The traffic sounds are muted by night, and the effect, as I walk along the long unlighted terrace, is of being in an unnatural and unknown place, walking on the moon on the dark side, an unknown atmosphere of moonlight chill and dark haze. Then you swing through a door and the dining room restores you to the lighted yellow-hued world.

Karachi
February 1953

Dearest Lili,

I've been a week here with Ben. The little plane from Delhi, an old DC3, flies at 7,000 feet, and all the deserts in the world seemed gathered beneath me – horizon to horizon the flat bare-boned land, then, far off, a flash of sea, and we land at Karachi. I leapt to Ben's arms, and off to discover this spare Pakistani world.

The air is warm! Wonderful after Delhi's cold. I like Karachi. But I like deserts, and if ever there was a roaring desert, Karachi is sitting on it!

Ben has taken rooms at a beach hotel, the top rooms overlooking a tidal swamp of mangrove. While he is wrestling with the forces of architecture I watch the tides swell in and out of the great mangrove forest. He rented a flat-bottomed twelve foot boat which we named 'Boat Achha', a play on a Hindi phrase meaning 'very good'. We sail and row in Boat Achha on week-ends and at the end of the day, when Ben comes home from the tensions of the work.

Last Saturday we sailed deep into the mangroves. The tide in the mangrove forests changes swiftly, and suddenly we felt it pouring out. We were in a mysterious swamp-scape out of sight of land. We sailed into a cross creek, and contorted grey roots twisted up from the yellow ooze rising into gnarled stumps. Ten feet above our heads their limbs and rudimentary leaves were bleached by ocean light, frosted by the salt of high tide. A mood of sea-death shut out all memory of land.

The boat slowed and we felt it drag and settle into the thick emulsion of the shallows. The oars were useless.

Ben jumped out, sinking to his thighs in mud. The boat didn't respond. 'You'll have to get out and help push. Hurry before we lose the tide.'

Horrified, I clambered into the waist-high slime. Slipping, pushing, we reached deeper water, and scrambled on board without capsizing. Ben opines that my tears had floated us. We could have had to wait until the next tide, with the boat ooze-glued, clinging to the contorted great roots through the night.

In those months of 1952 and 1953 we were frequently travelling between New Delhi and Karachi. Our first New Delhi flat had not worked out, and from the comfort of the Cecil Hotel Ben and I looked for a new home. We found a one-storey cottage with a small green garden in the Diplomatic Enclave, not as cosmopolitan as it sounded. We were almost in the country, the lots around us vacant, only a few buildings. We had the pleasure of birds and bees, a roof deck, and a garden to play with . . . And the delights of housekeeping – in India.

When men came to ask for bearer's work we campaigned against the caste system, insisting that they be willing to do the whole range of house-work. To make sure they understood, Ben led them to the bathroom and demonstrated the cleaning of the toilet. This instantly eliminated the applicants. They could not face the indignity. After a day of soul-searching one came back. We expected to love him although he was a driver and mechanic and we – without a car – needed a cook and bearer. But his charms melted with the pound of butter he made off with. Ben had a talk with the boy who burst into tears sobbing 'My first mistake, Sahib, such a small mistake.' We put him on probation, but he couldn't stand the shame of the theft, and the taunts of the neighboring sweepers who jeered at him for doing sweeper's work – like scabbing against a union. One night he packed and disappeared. Between trial servants I cooked – on an electric plate, and five miles to the groceries.

Our Indian friends from Karachi days, Jai Kumar and Ganga Atal, were appointed to Washington, D.C. They were allowed two or three servants by Government of India diplomatic rules. Majid, the young bearer we had known in Pakistan, had by now three children. If he'd leave his family with his parents the Atals would take him to America. An ardent family man, Majid refused the trip. Would we want Majid while they were away? We were between servants. We'd be glad to have him and gave up our crusade, hired a highly recommended cook, and a tiny cheerful toothless sweeper woman, Rati.

He was very personable, Majid. Handsome, with a swagger, and used to grand ways. When we parted him from his gold-banded bearer's turban – too pretentious for us – it confirmed his impressions of our small house. We were not the Big Americans he'd expected us to be. Since he was a mental giant with his powers untapped – lack of the slightest education meant lowly orders for him for life – Majid exercised his mind on immediate benefits. Never with the Atals – they were family to him; but here he worked diligently at outwitting me and at keeping Ben happy; a prerequisite of his strategy. And he was formidable. When he came he could speak no English and couldn't cook. When he left us two years later, he spoke very passable English and was a superlative cook. He turned out, single-handed, meals for thirty on our primitive charcoal stove. I taught him a few things and he took it from there. Being a strict Muslim, he didn't taste our food, but his seasonings were perfect – a mystery.

The cook, when Majid first came, was a Buddhist, of a caste of Burmese named Mogh – traditional bandits, who some hundred years ago reformed and became celebrated cooks. He was a very small young man with a pretty wife. They lived in one of our servant's quarters. Majid and his family had the other.

At first our cook often asked if we would get him 'Sister Bowe's heaven'. For months the mystery was unresolved, then we suddenly realized that he didn't like our village-style charcoal range and was yearning for the glories of his former employer, Ambassador Chester Bowles (Sister Bowe's) *oven*! The language problem! and a problem the servants managed better than I did.

The cook's wife was vivacious. Much of the time she swung coquettishly on the back lane gate chatting with delivery men, and local workmen. The cook didn't mind – a proof of his own self-esteem. Majid, a Muslim, kept his wife in deepest purdah, heavy curtains at the window and door. He had married her when she was eleven and he twenty; she was like both a wife and a daughter to him he said, so young when she came to his house.

She never left their little room, even in a burkah. The freedom of the cook's wife was an affront.

Early light edged the bedroom window shades; we were stirring, but still in half-sleep, when cries erupted in the courtyard. With one bound Ben was up and through the back door. 'What's going on here?' His voice had the three-dimensional quality it takes on, when he's out in force. 'Why you mad . . . Give me that knife! Let me in there, Rati. Now you two. Come to your senses! What do you have to say?'

I stayed out of it, alright, but could hear sobs, Rati talking excitedly, and in amazement, Majid's sobbing voice, 'Tried to kill me . . . ' 'So I see,' Ben said coldly, 'Why?'

The scene Ben had leapt into showed Majid cowering in a corner of the court, Rati, her wizened little frame pressed heroically against the kitchen screen door, holding in our ex-bandit cook who, brandishing a fourteen-inch knife I'd got him at his urging only the day before, struggled to break out and do Majid in.

The story came out. Majid had been advising the cook to lock up his wife. 'Like a brother,' sobbed Majid, 'try talk like a brother.' But the insinuations were too much for the cook and he was avenging her honor. They both quit on the spot and, forced to choose between them, for better or worse, we kept Majid.

From then on he was both cook and bearer and he liked the new responsibility. I am hopeless with servants and don't understand how to give orders, or how to see them carried out, to be kind and firm at once. 'You'll ruin him,' Ben warned me, 'unless you keep him under a firm hand.' But Majid had me buffaloed. I'd check his shopping arithmetic and the combination of pity at my addition, and injured dignity if I questioned anything, defeated me every time. I could see in his eyes that I had indeed ruined him. He became arrogant and at last, when finding me in an awkward situation, he laughed at me, I knew he was through. Ben liked Majid. Majid respected Ben. So it gratified me to observe the shrewd legalistically adroit way by which Majid, pacing the floor of our living room as we terminated his service, turned, point by point, the debt he owed us, an advance of Rs. 150, to our owing him Rs. 150. It was a beautiful display of intelligence that all three of us enjoyed. The bar missed a great advocate in Majid.

Young desert people of Rajasthan came into Delhi to do the hard construction work of the rapidly growing city. The women were colorful in red skirts gathered and flaring out to sometimes sixteen yards around the hem, the heavy silver ornaments and orange patterned shawls tossed loosely over their heads, swung gaily behind. The men wear *dhotis*, vests and turbans, colored turbans if their fathers are living, white if they themselves are the heads of their families.

They are very young and live and work close-knit like a tribe. They have the untamed quality of deer, gentle, edgey, a little wild. They work hard – hard labor in sun that may register 110F carrying bricks, stone and earth from before dawn to evening. The noon meal is a ball of lentil paste the size of a walnut, and a coarse *chapatti* – a flat disk of unleavened wheat bread. They drink the dirty water stored in construction tanks, tanks ten feet square and about four feet deep dug near the buildings they are working on.

Many are well under twenty; the just-married husbands and wives of poor desert communities. They leave the older people at home to herd goats, plant a little grain, and they come to the city to earn a few rupees a month to send to the village. After a year or two the whole crew may go back to the desert and another younger group come.

When a job begins they take bricks from the work and put up a village for themselves to live in. Huts in rows, grass roofs, a small shrine in the common center where at night they sing and dance. They are high-spirited, friendly and fierce, very handsome, small, slender, vital, often singing. Going home from work in the dark, the men sing, their strong eager voices welling from reserves undrained by their labors. In early morning before sun-up, walking through the cool half-light to the job, the women sing. They walk quickly, the pleated red skirts kicking out with each step, some carrying infants wrapped in dark cloth and swung over their shoulders like bags of grain, others are ready for imminent motherhood; children run bright-eyed and naked, shaved heads, the tiny girls with bracelets and anklets. Little girls are loved, but sons are the pride of India. The little sons walk ahead of everyone, very proud.

The Diplomatic Enclave was alive with the desert people. Foundations were going in just next door, and one morning I heard a surprising volume of laughs and talking. I looked out. The men worked away with grinning faces, but the women were crowded on a high mound of loose earth at one side of the lot. Bent forward they seemed to be supporting a young woman who stood awkwardly in the center with a stack of bricks on her head.

Our little old Rati was in the house; I sent her to see. She came back shaking her head. The woman, she said, was having a baby. Rati was very disapproving of those wild ones who won't go home and lie down for it. Having a baby with bricks on their head! Later Rati told me the baby died, and so did the mother.

One day the desert people began work in front of our house on a big field destined to become a public park. They were laying up small brick fences around each of the sapling trees to protect them from cows and goats. As I sat by the window writing I could see the women carry bricks on their heads, walking like Egypt in her double crown. In our garden, pink lagestroemia bloomed in the monsoon wind, sparrows clung to the bounding tree.

The men and women bent and straightened in the rhythm of their work, children played on the construction sandpiles, ran through puddles left by last night's rain. Some played by the storage tank leaning in to splash up the dirty water. A scene of laughing and chatter, fragments of song. Then, a woman's high voice struck my ear. Clear, high, repeating on a steady stinging note, a new extraordinary tone carried some message.

I looked out. The desert men were running from every direction towards the voice. Then the women dropped their loads from their heads, running from down the street to the field from over the way; everyone drawn by the voice. A message over and over. The running women took up the cry, breaking it in two over the woman's call . . .

I ran out toward the voice. Away down the road I could see the women gathered in, leaning together in a tense pulsing circle keening their high cry. Nearer the water tank the men crowded, bent down. I stopped. Rati caught up to me. 'What is it? What had happened?' 'Go back, Memsahib. I will see.' I walked slowly back and in a minute Rati came; The woman's little son had drowned in the tank.

All that day, as I sat writing at my desk by the window, I heard the women in their grief. The men had gradually returned to their work. The women freed the tragedy of its passion. Moving slowly in a cluster supporting the bereft mother, close-held. Their cry an arrow in the mind, they went from work site to work site, camp to camp. Their keening came to me changing, tempered by the variable wind. I remembered a doctor had said, 'You must cry often. Let out your grief. A wisdom we have lost is the ancient ritual of sharing, even of proclaiming, grief. That is the best healing.' My thoughts are playing with the quality of India, the quiet, woven with the joy and abandon of death; perhaps it is there also in the beauty and the rejection of the scales of its music; but more of this later.

We had a stimulating house-guest, a wild-eyed international food-planning expert, Ben's former teacher, E. A. A. Rouse, a charming Britisher, who kept us in mild uproar with Secretariat conferences and tales of universal famine ahead unless the world does something about it at once.

Projects were developing for me, too – an international show for the American Women's Club. I devised a difficult mixture of fabrics, crafts, costumes, dancers from each participating nation arranged in fan formation, named it 'A Tapestry of Nations' and hoped for the best – a high-style version in my mind – , but it was called by my friends a Patchwork of Nations. However my self-respect was rehabilitated by the successes of my furniture and fashion designs developed for Ben's Wool Pavilion for the International Industries Fair in 1955. The *Delhi News Circle* carried the account of our joint project:

AMERICAN COUPLE SET STAGE FOR INDIAN WOOL DISPLAY

On Divali the crowds queuing up outside the Wool Pavilion in the Indian Section of the Industries Fair got so thick that a big sign, hastily lettered, was hung at the entrance: 'Ladies only, or gentlemen accompanied by ladies, admitted.'

And what was it everybody wanted to see?

Well, as far as the unaccompanied, unadmissible gentlemen

went, the attraction just might have been the pretty models at the fashion shows (twice daily 6.30 and 8.30 p.m.). For many it was a look at the much discussed woolen clothes the models were showing – especially the jackets, capes and the like, purposely engineered to hang gracefully over sarees on chill winter evenings.

Others wanted to see the unusual pieces of furniture displayed along with carpets and woolen yard goods in the stalls of various manufacturers.

It also seems quite possible, guesses the architect who designed the building, that part of the crowd just wanted to get inside to find out exactly what was in the Pavilion – the only structure at the Fair without windows to provide a clue. Benjamin Polk was the architect. An American who has been practicing architecture in India for four years, Mr Polk was backed up on his Fair job for the International Wool Secretariat by his wife, Emily, who designed the interiors, the furniture, and the forty-five separate costumes in Indian wools for Indian women shown at the fashion shows.

This multiple project transformed our small house into a three-ringed circus. A troup of tailors inhabited our courtyard, cloth cuttings blew with every breeze, relays of girls, the daughters of friends for the most part – it was an achievement to have pursuaded their parents to let them have their daily fittings and to model in this commercial show. The show was dignified and lovely; I had insisted on classical music, rather than the expected popular. The musician would not permit himself to be seen – the commercial aspect again – and sat in a room built for him. And the tussles with furniture men! I designed every piece, cut every garment, chose and trained the models . . . lost ten pounds. The construction was so slow we despaired until, awake at three one morning the thought struck – Irene! Would she, would she consider *supervising*? We were over there at daybreak. 'Think of your village! There'd be money in it for your village!' This argument she couldn't resist!

All day Irene strode through the muck, sat on wet brick walls, knitted, made coffee for us, worried about the coolies, pushed the work ahead. I stayed on the job nights to 3 a.m. devising ways to hoist fifteen-foot-square carpets, installing experimental furniture and displays. And we made the deadline. One of four in the entire Fair to open on time, and visited on opening day by Prime Minister Nehru.

My work on ancient Indian furniture and household forms received another push when the American Women's Club asked if I would give a program on interior decoration for one of the Indian girls' colleges. Did they want pelmets and flounces? Well, no, perhaps something to do with using Indian objects in a modern house. I made, instead, an appeal that they rediscover their own forms for today, and I backed it up with my research on those forms. I drew reconstructions of ancient rooms from the Vedic Period 1500 B.C., the Gupta Period 300 A.D. and the lavish Medieval Period 1000 A.D.. Colored vividly, the pictures were thrown by epidiascope on a large screen. The great sigh of delight that greeted the reconstructions convinced me I'd won converts. I hadn't; but ideas were further crystalized, and happening to describe them to our friend Pyarelal Nayar he immediately said he would like the President of India to hear about them.

Pyarelal had been the private secretary to Mahatma Gandhi during the last ten years of Gandhi's life. He lived in a small suite of rooms at Connaught Circus with his tiny wife Bela Devi, from Bengal. During the terrible partition riots, the East Bengal area of Noakali saw frenzied killings. The entire population had gone mad with fear. Neighbors were in death struggles, appeals to reason useless. Gandhi feared that continuation of the carnage would lead to even worse disasters elsewhere and set out on foot with Pyarelal and a few followers to try by the force of his presence to bring sanity. They found refuge at the house of Bela Devi's father. And his calming of the volcano at Noakali is one of the great sagas of his life.

We often climbed the narrow stairs to their small door, banged the brass knocker, stepped over the door sill, which was ten inches high giving a fillip of discovery to the terraced, staired and vine-hung rooms of Pyarelal and Bela Devi. Sometimes Pyarelal read us a chapter he was drafting for his mammoth biography of Gandhi, *The Last Years*. He would ask Ben's opinion on the clarity of some points. He had a rare quality of quiet.

I think of Pyarelal steadily compiling the minutiae of those last tremendous years, think of him sitting in the shadowy corner of his retreat, sturdy legs curled under him on the big white cloth laid smoothly on the floor, the fan whirling overhead fanning the leaves of plants trained through the window into the white room, and fresh jasmine flowers laid on the low table around the picture of Gandhi. Warmth and quietness and humour. One had a feeling of the whole apartment smiling. They enjoyed cooking paralyzingly hot food, and (with unpeppered dishes prepared beforehand) would give us the hot stuff as if that was to be our meal. As we gasped at a nibble they would feign amazement and said they would see if there was something else. Bela Devi, tiny as a bird, would come laughing into the room carrying a special and delectable meal for us. Pyarelal told me there were three degrees of chili peppers; those that burned you, those that stunned you, or those that knocked you out. He liked the latter.

From the great days with Gandhi, Pyarelal knew Dr Rajendra Prasad, now President of India. He had access to the President as an old friend, and was so interested in my work in developing indigenous furniture forms – rather rediscovering the indigenous Indian form and letting it replace the foreign surroundings currently prevalent in homes – that he asked if I would come with him one evening to tell the President about it. The private rooms of the President were to be done over, and Pyarelal thought that my work would be suitable for that redecoration.

Pyarelal had a jeep. An old Willys war-surplus beast. We went, he and I, in this vehicle to call on the President of India. Parked it among the limousines of State, were ushered down crimson carpets past sumptuous rooms, once the Viceregal suites of British India, into the farthest reaches of Sir Edwin Lutyens's magnificent Viceroy's Palace – now carefully called a House – the President's House, the Rajtrapati Bhavan, a great building of red and buff sandstone, the architectural climax of Lutyens's fine work. The President of India had chosen humble rooms in a back corridor for his private use.

There were no guards at the door. We were expected, and a bearer, probably a family servant by his un-chic look, let us in. Dr Prasad had been reading, sitting on an old-fashioned half-backed chaise-longue upholstered with chintz roses. Yards and yards of the chintz, printed solid with red roses, big ones, on a whitish ground, covered the chaise, the bulky overstuffed chairs, and the footstools. And the same chintz hung in a solid sweep of curtains beside the eighteen-foot windows. The walls, ceiling, doors, ceiling fans and fireplace screen were painted dark green.

As we came in, the President got up, folded his hands in the gracious gesture of Indian greeting and sat down. I had brought my writing and drawing, but looking into the deep patient face of this man, it all seemed trivial, like presenting a tap routine to amuse a saint. I wanted to vindicate Pyarelal for his interest, and so with the nervous brashness of self-depreciation, I flipped through my work, weeping inside at the disservice I was doing to the idea, myself, and Pyarelal. Dr Prasad took the work away from me and quietly went through it. He may have seen my difficulty. He then told me that his rooms were to be redone. I had been prompted that the President cannot make a request but can accept or reject, so now I said that I would like to study his rooms and present drawings to show how they might reflect these ideas. He nodded and smiled and approved my doing that. A moment of conversation with Pyarelal, and we left.

The jeep broke down on the road beyond the gates. As long as we were going down hill, we could push, but once on the flat we stopped. Night had fallen with cold mist. I was chilly and apprehensive of the task I'd undertaken. No one came to help, no taxi; at last a tonga came and I trotted off to call the garage for Pyarelal. When Pyarelal's two-volume work came out, he drove out to us in his jeep to bring us our autographed copy, a signal honor and touch of friendship.

I began my investigations of forms, pored over old books and monographs, made detailed sketches of museum displays that, even if showing a mere suggestion of furniture, gave a clue to a past form. I went to Calcutta where I spent days sketching at the Museum. In the depths of Orissa I had studied the temples and came back with notes and plans. Immediately the flu attacked me. The Military Officer in charge of the President's House telephoned regularly, where was the material, what was I doing? And it *was* much too long before I presented my work. When I did I felt that a profound misunderstanding had developed between the Military Officer and me. At our first meeting he looked sternly at me. 'What do you want for doing this work?' I was so surprised that I simply smiled feebly, 'I'm not sure what you mean,' 'When you are, we can talk again. Thank you for coming.' At last the work was ready. I had drawn up and colored what I hoped would be rooms expressing the President's needs and purposes. But I was not permitted to present the volume myself. The Military Officer allowed me to give it into his own keeping. Later I heard that an Indian woman had been chosen to redesign the room. It was better that way, for many reasons. And eventually I will do a volume on this aspect of Indian design.

4
The Heart of India
1955

When Ben decided we should go in August for our holiday, everyone said 'No one else will be travelling, it's out of season.' Not a time for tours; but we must see the heart of India, the land south of the Jumna and the Ganga rivers. We had to know what was hidden in the magnetic center of that land.

With our luggage piled in the Harpalpur station yard we looked for the bus we would take to Chhatarpur – City of the Royal Umbrella. We could not read the Hindi letters and crowds of people who had surged off the train with us filled the fleet of old buses before we had found the station master and had asked which one was ours.

A young blind man stood beside me as I waited. His *dhoti* and shirt were neat and he carried his belongings in a blue cloth. He hoped to board a bus just ahead of us but wasn't sure where it was. No one realized his difficulty in the rush. Porters banged into him and shouted. Passengers pushed him. No resentment or tension came into his face, only a slight moving of his lips, and of his fingers on the blue bundle. He went slowly toward the bus which loaded from the back. At last he joined the crowd that waited at one side. In front of him a man bent down to look into a piece of luggage. The blind man found the shelf made by the bent back, and set his small burden down on it. After a moment of gentle, amused explanations by the others the blind man lifted off his bundle. Just then a porter carrying a mountain of luggage on his head careened past. Someone took the arm of the blind man and pulled him out of the way. Instantly at this touch of help the moving lips of the blind man curved into a smile. It was remarkably like the smile that hovers over the faces of ancient Hindu and Buddhist sculptures. Perhaps it comes from accepting an unseen world.

The approach to Chhatarpur was through rolling broken land; rich land, irrigated from the earliest times by small natural catchpools and stone *bunds*, or dams. Even in the outskirts it was apparent that the town had a leisurely graceful atmosphere, unlike the overcrowded cities of the north. It was the administrative center of the District where the exotic former Maharaja of Chhatarpur used to have his family palaces and the seat of his Government. Now, the driver said, the new Maharaja lives at Khajuraho.

The bus whirled into the station yard. We got down and immediately a tall Sikh with a carefully wrapped turban and well-groomed beard rolled neatly into a hair net, came up to us.

'If you are going to the traveller's bungalow,' he said, 'this bus will take you there for two rupees house charge.'

The bus was empty by now and baggage was being noisily lowered from the top into waiting hands. When it was all down but ours, the driver, the Sikh, two porters and four or five wellwishers got into the back. A tall thin boy about fifteen years old started to climb in with them. He was not like the others. They wore conventional Western clothes, he wore a long green shirt that flapped about his thin bare legs. A strange green. It was dark and light at the same time, pale and bright, faded and also very intense. The boy's hair was long and thick, sculptured around the curves of his thin face. He had wide urgent eyes, delicate neck and shoulders. He swung up to the back of the bus. The others shouted at him, and someone pushed him off. The bus began to move and as we gained speed the boy leapt on to the back runningboard with a defiant look. Three men rushed at him but he clung to the hand rail, teeth clenched, eyes stabbing at the men. As they broke his hold and threw him to the ground, he cried out 'Work! Work! I want to work.'

The Sikh saw that I was watching and explained, 'He wants to unload your luggage but we have our own men.'

The bus went along on a road that ran under high cliffs. Then we made a hairpin turn through a gate and climbed a gardened hillside to the top where a pleasant bungalow was maintained by the State. From here one could see the sweep of the countryside and town.

Our luggage was brought down quickly and taken into the

house and as we turned to go inside the boy in the green shirt came around the corner of the house. He had apparently climbed the steep cliff that dropped from the bungalow to the highway below, he was breathing hard. A glance showed him that he was too late. On one side of the driveway was a large stone. Walking to it he sat down and rested his chin on his hands to watch the last bag disappear inside, to watch the men get into the bus and drive away. Then he got up, and, moving slowly, disappeared around the cliffside.

'Do you live here in Chhatarpur?' we asked the driver.

'Yes, I own this bus. The Maharaja owns the other buses.'

'Do you know the Maharaja?'

'Know him, he's like a father to me; I came a young man. He likes me. I manage his buses for him.' The Sikh flashed his pleasant smile at us. He spoke English well and was enjoying the conversation.

'Have you always lived here?' we asked as we reached the bottom of the hill. He made the motor hum around the turn.

'No, I came from Jubbulpore. An uncle here.'

We suddenly realized that we had turned away from the direction of the station.

'Where are we going, the bus station is back there.'

He laughed, pleased to have surprised us. 'The bus is coming to a crossroad down this way where it must stop. I have arranged everything for you. It is more pleasant than the station.'

In a few minutes we coasted over the crossroad and stopped beside a row of tumbling houses and a tea shack. On the ground sat a lively old woman selling vegetables. Several old men sat near joking with her. They would exchange remarks then throw back their heads in high laughter. She shook her head until the big brass loops in her ears whirled wildly. She rearranged the faded red saree over her hair with quick wrinkled hands, sold a cucumber, all on a chain of cheerful comment. She was minutely wrinkled, her mouth was bare of teeth but her charm was magnetic and the thin tired old farmers were pleased.

Nearby was an open fronted tea shack with a door at the back leading into a dark room. A small, bent, bald-headed man wearing a belted shirt sat in the center of the floor facing a woman who leaned out of the door. Her thin face, pale as a half-seen carving in the shadows of a cave, was tired and almost stupid with poverty or ignorance or illness or all of them. Her features were delicate, her eyes large, her skin very light. She seemed to carry a remnant of an ancient grace, but was starved, and not just physically, to a level lower than most hungry people, possibly because of her depths of sensitivity. She stood looking down with a loose smile at the bent man. There seemed to be something wrong with him, he cowered down over his crossed legs, then throwing his arms up, shook and swung himself, grunting and babbling with imbecile speech. He began to scoot along the floor with his arms stretched toward her. She listlessly motioned for him to go away, and disappeared through the dark door way.

The bus for Khajuraho stopped in front of us. We changed over to it and waited for the shifting of the luggage.

The babbling man from the tea shack scrambled to his feet and, clutching a small bag against his body, sidled with rolling furtive eyes toward the bus. He was not old but was lined and seared by affliction. As he neared the bus, he began to grunt.

The Sikh swung himself into the driver's seat.

'Will you drive this, too?'

'Only a few miles to the district station.'

He noticed the grunting man.

'That man can't talk, he's mute. There are two mutes in Chhatarpur.' Suddenly the man broke into a scream. He ran back and forth on the road, babbling and screaming and looking down the road. Up the road came an old man in a loin cloth. We heard him, 'Aah ah – ha – ah – ah.' The other mute! The younger man grimaced and ran away, then came back, whining. As they met the old man was quiet, but his eyes were excited. The passengers on the bus watched them intently, laughing and leaning over to see. The two men walked away together. The Sikh laughed, 'The two mutes together.'

Beyond Chhatarpur the occasional rock outcroppings which we had seen all the way began to loom into crags, hills and low plateaus. The fields around them were flat and green, the earth soft red. Clumps of trees conferred together, or leaned confidingly against the stone ridges. Wind, sun and chiselling rain had removed the softer layers of rock, carving the cliffs in strong horizontal lines crossed at intervals by vertical fissures and set-back surfaces. Rising from the flat green tree-scattered plain these intricate hills, their foundations hidden by gathered trees, have force and majesty beyond their size. They are small mountains rather than hills. A tranquillity lay here . . . a seen tranquillity . . . hills like waterlilies spicing a still green lake . . . like lilies on an ashram lake 'born' as the Atharva Veda says 'of the sweat of laboring disciples'. This must surely be the *ashrama* country, the monastery zone, the sacred 'Neutral Belt of No War', established in India about 1500 B.C.

Back in Delhi, I had taken notes from translations of the epic poem, the Ramayana, about the southern Gangetic country. 'After defeat, the King Visva Mitra with his queen went to the south and engaged in religious training'; ' . . . the southern districts . . . safe for monasteries'; ' . . . the south is the home of religious study for the Ramanic age' – and 'south', here, is clearly the country south of the Ganges. 'The region south of the Jumna was in Rama's day full of great monasteries.'

We were on the threshold of that region.

The guide books, buttering their bread with commercial jam, ignore it or don't know it. Our friends had said it was somewhere near Allahabad, the ancient city of Prayaga, where the two rivers meet.

The road taking us into this discovery was rough and curved. The Sikh feeling power in his hands hastened the decision of loitering cows, plunged the bus full speed toward them, guessed their intention instantly, and swung round them without a change of speed.

'This is the road to Khajuraho and this is the police station. I get down here,' the Sikh said turning into a side road and stopping. 'The other driver will be along soon.' We shook hands.

He strode across to the compound gate and walked up the sidewalk. He had the typically prideful walk of Sikh men.

Originally the Sikhs were pacifist theologists combining Islamic and Hindu principles, and preaching that all men are brothers and that God is one, but after Moghul persecution they stepped to the Hindu side and welded themselves into a militant, disciplined and distinctive group. With dense black beards and eyebrows, black compelling eyes, and monumental turbans, these men are impressive, and the most magnificent woman I have ever seen was a Sikh bride.

Here is a hush . . . the earth's life lies buried under the surface. In this land of mid-India the pace is slow. There is the still rim of the pool where men have come, over the centuries, to evolve, in isolated settlements, or ashrams, their studies and meditations in the Hindu sciences of life.

The ancient Vedic writings say that Brahma, the God of gods, the Immortal Creator, at the request of the gods who were alarmed at the lack of discipline in men, produced from his own intelligence a 100,000 chapters in dharma, the science of religion; artha, the science of governing; and kama, the science of love.

The great kingdoms of the Kurus and the Panchalas that 3,000 years ago ruled the tongue of land between the Ganga and the Jumna was the well of Vedic learning from which all India came to drink. The Veda said that in addition to pre-eminence in the first two sciences the 'Panchala country appears to have been the part of India where the science of erotics was specially cultivated'. The borders of this kingdom were less that a hundred miles from the quiet plain we drove through, a passive plain that longed for the creative energies of men, that waited receptive, like 'the supreme immanent primal essense conceived of as a woman'.

We approached a grove of trees scattered to circle broad fields of grass and we felt that a temple should be here, a pinnacle reaching up through the trees. Yes, a dark shape. I turned to the driver, 'Khajuraho?' He nodded.

We drove on about a half mile to the traveller's bungalow. I sink into a chair, still the quiver inside from long travelling. How quiet it is; a few bird voices; steps crisp on gravel. The bus roar in my ears is subsiding. Clean cold water to wash in. Tea has come. How good the tea smells. How good it is to be quiet.

We were thinking of the temples. 'I thought they'd be larger.'

We felt the temples standing for a thousand years of afternoons in a recess of history, built by the medieval Chandela kings, who are believed to have brought to Khajuraho the master craftsmen of the Orissa cycle. They kept the secret sciences of love and wrought them into temples with the last strength of medieval India.

The sky had cleared and a late sun was shining. 'Shall we walk over there after tea? Perhaps see just one this afternoon?'

Fatigue discouraged me, but I must go to see. 'Yes, let's go.'

We turned into the road. A bird hidden in a roadside tree whistled at us, long notes that slid up the scale and down, clear and ridiculing. A young farmer came toward us with a pole over his shoulder. He wore a small brass earring in one ear lobe. Cows came up the road. Small, self-possessed cows with feminine eyes. They walked one behind the other followed by a little naked boy who carried a long thin stick with which he tapped the flanks of the last cow.

We turned back to the high grass, the trees, the silent late day, and the four dark temples. There were others, smaller satellites. There were tall dark temples crouched like lions on square mountains at the corners of the field. There were guardian trees; there was the broad field and those four magnetic temples. The path was a shadow in the tall grass, the temples were tall shadows in the corners of the sky.

Which one shall we see first? Which gate to heaven? There are four. The near one? The middle ones? No, the far one. Time to think about it, and to walk. To feel the sun, the brushing grass, to enter the mental vestibule of an event.

At the middle of the field a path broke away toward the far corner. At this point in the field the temples were equally distant. Here was a calm, a peaceful center, a point where the pull of each was nullified by the others, as somewhere in the universe there must be an eternal void, all gravities being joined to produce a space of no attraction, a happy vacuum where fortunate particles drift in a millennial ease, unwanting.

Like the others the temple on the left stood on a high stone terrace and seemed set apart from the temporal earth. Walking toward it, all sense of its size had vanished. This building was beyond size. At this distance one could see in some detail the tall roof forms clustered together, reaching in successive thrusts like fountains, like mountain peaks, like desire; cavish balconies that pierced the mountain; the stone lion that pawed the middle air above cliffs of sinuous sculpture, strata of stone flesh.

We reached the broad steep terrace steps. An efficient blue and white metal sign – 'Please Remove Your Shoes' – was fastened to a step. Whatever the consideration, religious or archeological, removing one's shoes to walk with bare feet on the stone was right. In shadow the stone was cool, in sun, warm. It was uneven and our escaped feet moulded themselves to the stone's rhythm. We were no longer strangers sailing stiffly in shoe boats over the temple, but fish in its waves, children of the stone, responsive, and intimate. The temple was alive underfoot. To whirl and leap on the broad stone platform would have been natural. But we began slowly to walk.

We walk, the temple dances. We stand still, the temple revolves its sculptured glories before us. The sun's bright tongue licks their round bodies. Warm ivory-stone gods embrace their goddesses in an eternal moment of exquisite passion, express in the very act of supreme delight the serene face of self knowledge, the two-edged transforming joy of discovering the seed of the tree of life while eating its fruits.

Eyes were not enough to grasp at once this vivid pattern and its relation to the uplifting whole. The horizontal elements, as in the cliffs of the countryside, pointed to the vertical. The vertical lifted continuously away in powerful upward surges. We looked east toward the half visible hills. If we understood those hills, we would understand the temples. We walked to the edge of the platform and looked back at the building.

From here one could begin to comprehend the mastery of sculptural form that the creators of these monuments possessed. The power of the building leapt through the stones. The stones and craftsmen had become incidental to the building, as if with vitality and strength and identity, it had always existed; as if each stone had been pulled up into a place in the sky by the desire of the temple to create itself, to clothe itself, to be visible to other eyes.

The intrigues of shadow and light had been subtly transformed over a thousand years by black lichen, so that, to the already complex was added further complexity. The light places – exposed ridges – were made dark and their undersides which would originally have been shadow, being protected from rain and therefore lichen, remained light, thereby deceiving the reasonable eye into seeing what could not be – light shadow.

With profound architecture like this, action of the time element is a pulse of its life. Through this action it lives, develops tranquilly throughout ages, silently changes with the centuries revealing depths that were only a dream to the architect. Through this action the architect lives immortally at his work, fulfilling, exploring, and changing.

The sun was near the horizon. 'Let's look at the inside before it's too dark.'

The entrances to the temples face east. Carved steps mount up into the body of the building. The first rays of morning sun would penetrate into the inner sanctum, and touch the stone godhead. At the passage to the entrance a heavy smell lay on the air. I was puzzled.

'What is that peculiar smell?'

'It's from bats.'

I looked at the ceiling. The carved recesses of stone lace had been cleaned and screened but were indelibly stained to an oily black by centuries of use by bats. Layers of narrowing stone circles, cut into intricate designs, enclosed a black opening. A concept of deep mystery. Cities of bats must have thrived there.

At the end of the long balconied corridor the entrance door stood like a carved fabric shadow. As we stepped through it, the reek of bats completely enveloped us. When our eyes adjusted to the dark, we saw that we were in a square room. Opposite the entrance door was the secret inner shrine. The side walls of the room carried low-roofed balconies at window level admitting traces of light. Four powerful columns upheld the center ceiling which as in the passage was an overlay of elaborately carved stone strata which surrounded a throbbing black void.

The whole space above the floor – walls, columns, ceiling, balconies – was peopled with stone figures. Gods and goddesses stood gracefully together. Exquisitely modelled women clinging to sinuous stone trees, leaned toward us.

We walked quickly between the animated walls of the narrow ambulatory that circled the sanctum. The fading light filtered into the west balcony and revealed a multitude of stone bodies hovering around us. They were close and seemed to crowd us.

As I stood there I suddenly was overwhelmed by the power of this building. I was aware of the tons of stone poised in the thrusting roofs over my head, of the welling symbolic energy that swept like a petrified river around us, of the high fragile stairs and the narrow vulvic passage that were all that linked us to the familiar earth, of this dark room and its secret inner shrine guarding a seed of the pervading deity.

I was in a mountain, hiding under its cliffs, crags, and staccato breasts, hiding under an internal sky, hiding in a dry caldron.

I was in a mountain carved by living men who gave their life to stone then borrowed it back again. Perhaps I had walked up disappearing stairs, through a passage that had closed behind me, through a narrow grasping door and into a womb of stone, a sepulchre. I felt dizzy as if there were no air.

'Let's get out of here, it's too dark.'

At the top of the stairs we stood for a moment between the light sky and the earth where night was blowing like smoke across the fields. We went down into the darkness, into the black, emerald, and red amber of Indian evening earth. The far temples seemed to have come ominously alive. I felt pursued and hurried along the path. I watched the ground in front of me intently, a pretense of careful walking, but it was from reluctance to see what might be behind. As we passed the temple near the gate, I glanced toward it and noticed a small single-roof pergola with a stone creature caught up in it. It seemed terribly like something trapped.

We went through the gate, out into the road and toward the bungalow. The flat surface of the road reflected some of the sky's light. As we walked quickly along, we saw coming toward us a large grey bull. He came with high steps, and tossed his head in the air as though in agitated search. I realized that I had expected him, the animation of the temple come to meet us on the road. We went to the right to avoid him. He suddenly saw the men and bullocks who were still at work in the field to the left and, wheeling, plunged down the small embankment and raced over to his harnessed brothers.

The hawk cuckoo of India is a bird famous in classics and in folk-lore not only for its cuckolding habits but for its powerful and translatable voice. Every local language has its own interpretation and to the Englishman it said with an emphasis he felt, 'Oh Lord, oh Lord, how very hot it's getting. We feel it, we feel it, we feel it!!!' This last with demonic passion. One of these birds discovered us at the traveller's bungalow. At dawn he stationed himself in the large tree outside our window and railed at us for lying abed. First, a low doleful comment on the passage of time, sung slowly up and down the scale, 'Oh Lord, oh Lord, how very late it's getting.' Then as our indifference became unbearable he screamed 'They're sleeping, they're sleeping, they're sleeping' until the last ascending word pierced the shattered sound barrier in our ears and we sat up thoroughly awake and astonished at such lung-power. By now the enormity of it had become an obsession with him. The bird who had got up at dawn from the shell on resented our easy ways. The resentment hardened into self-righteousness and our slothful life enraged him. Since he was impossible to ignore we decided to get up.

As the sun swings through the summer noon all work stops. At this time of day, India regains an ancient silence. Small domestic birds sit in the deepest shadows, night prowlers are asleep in caves or under bushes, dogs and cows rest under the trees. High in the fierce sky kites, vultures and eagles sweep with minimum effort, leaning along the cool currents of the upper air. Everyone who can, stays indoors and sleeps through the terrible midday hours.

But after an early lunch we put on our white cotton hats, spread our black umbrella and went out to see the temples in the noonday sun. We hurried over the hot road, pulled toward them by the elation of rediscovery. They would be changed in this new light.

At the side of the protected area we crawled through the wire fence to another of these vibrant structures. We went up the steps and took off our shoes. The stones burned our feet so we went immediately inside.

Many of the figures had been taken from the inner room and corridors. The brackets and columns seemed bare and forsaken, and although the proportions were pleasant it was apparent that the essence of these rooms had been in their exuberant sculptures. Without them the light was dead like light filtering through the water of a stagnant pool.

As we came out to the top of the steps we saw that two boys stood in the deep grass below the platform watching us. They began to climb the steep side of the plinth, pulling themselves up from one irregularity in the stones to another. They climbed with astonishing ease, a familiarity with gravity that carried them like lizards up a wall, that would have carried them over the temple itself, shown them hidden places in convolutions of the top that only the builders and the birds had seen. In their blood perhaps, the stone carvers dreamed and they climbed by memory. By the time we were down on the platform the boys stood at its edge looking at us. Suddenly we faced them. They backed away, turned, sauntered to the edge, dropped down as they had come up and walked through the long grass not once looking back.

A man was vigorously rubbing the base-stones of a neighboring temple. He straightened up and smiled as we approached.

'How do you like the temples?' he asked politely.

He was a young man, slight and scholarly with heavy eye-glasses resting on his slender prominent nose. His fresh white shirt hung loose over his white *dhoti*, and his cuffs were turned carefully back. He held a small brush in his right hand and in his left a thin rubber hose that was attached to a bucket with a pump on top.

We smile back at him. 'The temples are wonderful. Are you in charge here?'

'I'm with the government's archeological staff here. There are five of us. We are engaged in restoration experiments.'

'What are you doing now?' we asked looking at the equipment.

'I am removing the black lichen with pure water. We have tried many things, but it has been found that pure water is the best solvent.'

The stone he had rubbed was clean and pale yellow, the adjoining stones were streaked with black.

'But the black is attractive on the yellow stones,' I commented heretically, 'and it's been there so long. Do you expect to take all of it off?'

'Oh, yes, it eats into the stones and they will eventually disintegrate.'

'But for a thousand years . . . ' The temples are remarkably intact . . . an astonishment to the first Englishmen who 'found' them upright and unviolated in the jungle scrub. But it was no use arguing about it. Progress had arrived. At his present rate with his brush and bucket of purest water he would be another thousand years at the job and new lichen could fill in behind him. We left him happily experimenting with his time eradicator, went down into the grass and off in the direction of the far right temple.

Here was a small open plinth that stood in front of the temple. It supported a monolithic stone animal, a huge bull lying comfortably on his platform. His neck was garlanded with stone jewelry, chains of mute stone bells, and his forehead adorned with a stone pendant. His great smooth sides were sleekly polished. And there we saw the mark of the vandal – hacked into the stone were the letters D.H.R. We felt ashamed and unbelieving as if through negligence we were partly responsible for the crime. It was apparent that nothing could be done about it since to rework the side of the figure would be to change the form and destroy the remarkable finish of the stone.

The bull was a charming beast, so gentle and responsive that it could easily be loved. I stroked his stone neck, it was wonderfully smooth and endearing. It was easy to imagine the garlands of marigolds hung about his neck, children climbing up to straddle the broad back and to slide shouting down the long sides, and unhappy people leaning for comfort against his round body. It is a surprise to Westerners to discover that Indian cattle are friendly. They are what people expect them to be and the bulls wander serenely on crowded sidewalks, steal turnips out of the vegetable seller's basket and are gently pushed out of the way by pedestrians. After several thousand years of affection they are as domesticated as dogs, and more peaceable.

By seeing this lovable stone bull sitting alone in his small temple, undisturbed by centuries of passing worldly events or by the forgotten hands that wounded his side, one begins to understand that cattle represent to the Hindu his protective relationship with the entire brotherhood of animals and one begins to appreciate more fully the vision of Isaiah.

'The wolf also shall dwell with the lamb, and the leopard shall lie down with the kid; and the calf and the young lion and the fatling together; and a little child shall lead them. And the cow and the bear shall feed; their young ones shall lie down together: and the lion shall eat straw like the ox. And the sucking child shall play on the hole of the asp, and the weaned child shall put his hand on the cockatrice' den. They shall not hurt nor destroy in all my holy mountain: for the earth shall be full of the knowledge of the Lord, as the waters cover the sea.'

To us the idea is sentimentally or heroically symbolic. India is, at least, a vegetarian world.

We walked across the field to the little pergola we had seen the night before. Like the large temples it stood on its own terrace with steep steps rising to a square open space covered by an intricate pyramid roof held up by heavy columns. Almost filling, almost bursting out of the space stood the gigantic black granite figure of a boar, perhaps ten feet long. His massive head lifted high, he stood on a platform and straddled the long sinuous body of a worshipping stone serpent.

The idea of encompassing divinity had guided the sculptor – the tusks had become spirals, the muscles of the powerful legs had evolved into women and serpents, the rough texture of the colossal body was expressed by a formal design of gods and goddesses carved row after row over his entire back and sides. Standing in the pergola beside it one cannot see the whole of it and had to understand by the universe of detail, as with our own universe. We were astonished at this undescribed masterpiece. It should be studied and made known.

We walked onto the field, stood in the shade of the large temple and looked up at it. The surprising thing about ancient buildings anywhere is that they were made with hands, normal-sized hands attached to normal-sized men, though they seem to have been built by men as tall as trees who carried the massive stones as we would bricks, laid them carefully together, and pushed the columns into line as we might straighten the legs of a table. Or they were made by magicians who conjured them out of the upper air. But an architect is a kind of magician. He sees a thing that isn't there, and makes it appear, and when it has appeared it becomes more than the men who made it.

We sat down there in the shade on the temple terrace and leaned back on our elbows. The high point of the heat was passed and the air was pleasant. We put our hats under our heads and lay full length looking up at the cliffs of sculpture. A sparrow bustled through the air, perched impudently on the headdress of a goddess and stared sharply down at us. We pivotted the umbrella on its handle and pointed it at the sparrow who stuttered, then flew away.

In the afternoon about three o'clock, our last afternoon at

Khajuraho, we left the shelter of the bungalow and walked down the road for a final visit to the temples. We took paper and pencils with us this time because it was apparent from the photographs we had seen, that the quality of the buildings had been difficult to capture in a cold camera eye. Maybe it would be just as difficult with a warm pencil but we could try.

Again we passed the near temple, went straight ahead, entered through the narrow gate, and walked toward the center of the field. I felt wonderfully alert and detached, as though I had never been there before but carried with me a clear pre-knowledge, a coin whose two faces were memory opposed to surprise. I tried to see around me with more than physical sight, to understand the extra dimension that had been created here. Since then I have wondered how much of the strange spirit of Khajuraho filters through to visitors. Not what we see: we all know stones. Not just the temples: we've seen travelogues of temples. Not the grass. Just as with a poem, it cannot be described. The description of a poem is the poem itself.

We walked down the steps, to a tree that shaded a bit of higher ground just south of the center of the field and sat down. The sweet smell of grass being crushed under us filled the air. We leaned back against the trunk and began to draw the Kandariya Temple. There was no near sound but the hiss of the pencil sliding over the paper. There was no near time and no near space. We sat there pleasantly forever.

I could imagine a life in this open field weightless in wonder. But pitch no tent, build no house. See new daily shadows rise with the sun, milk moonlight from night cows, comb fruit from branches, bake effortless bread on a hot flat stone.

I leaned over and pulled a stem of grass out of its tubestalk to taste the tender part. To my surprise I saw that a small, perfectly black star-shaped flower quivered on the stem. This is the flower of the great Khajuraho.

Behind me in the bus for Chhatarpur women and their little children crowded cozily together, a gay potpourri of sarees, silver jewelry and near-naked babies.

A young women was nursing her infant. It was so small that it was almost hidden in her saree. She was a plain girl with a rather large nose and a rectangular face but at the moment she had a remarkably beautiful expression. She had abandoned herself to the sensation in her breast – her head up, lips parted, eyes half closed looking in upon the pulses of her body. She hardly held the baby but let it lie on her lap and leaned so that the full dark fruit of her breast hung with its purple stem in the infant's mouth. She was completely unaware of where or who she was, unaware that I looked at her, that there were other people all around her.

When the driver jumped down at a stop the three-year-old boy in the section behind me banged on the back of the driver's seat and stared at the steering wheel until his mother lifted him over to stand in the seat. Then he slowly rested one minute hand on the wheel, and turned around to look ecstatically into his mother's face. Any little boy in the machine age.

As we travelled I searched the countryside for its events – animals asleep on rocks, delphinium birds (blue wheels that turn the air), but we went too fast, always too fast, even an inept thirty miles an hour is too fast. Walking is the right pace to see the world move past itself, reveal the dark by the bright. Eyes grasp the outsides of things, memory images the inside, but the sounds that accompany sights are drowned by a categorical need for speed.

At Harpalpur station the porters had new, dazzling red shirts and red turbans, the usual city-station porter's uniform. This bright red is a wonderful color for serious clothes. In the solemn shadows of Westminster Abbey, the clerical robes make one's heart leap. The red glows like live color. It adds to the mysterious height of the half-seen vaults, it deepens the ringing choir-voice echoes and centers your eye so that the whole vast stone cathedral seems to exist solely to cherish this spark of vibrant red. Out here on this little crowded platform it transformed an otherwise disorganized scene into a ballet. The men rushed about and you saw the other people in their position relative to the four red dancers.

To the left of the passengers' shelter I caught sight of a flash of red. Large straw bales were being wrestled off a truck, weighed, and then lined up by the track for loading. A porter juggled them from the truck, onto the scales, and then into loading position. His white *dhoti* rolled into pleats about his legs as he worked. He had pushed his red sleeves high on his arm, and wrapped his red turban to tilt to one side of his head. In the exposed ear swung a small gold earring. He moved like a dancer, and his face, full of daring, was a dancer's face. He flung himself through his strenuous work with the stylized grace of high art. There was the repetition, the repetition and change, the precision of balance in the midst of whirling controlled movement, complete mastery of his body and the bulky counterweight. And for stage there was the shock of red weaving itself through straw and grey and white under a spotlight sun.

I noticed a woman sidle around the corner of the building and walk uncertainly through the crowd. She was very small and had pulled the end of her transparent pale yellow saree over her head so that only her dark eyes showed between the saree's gold-tinsel borders. To protect herself from the dust of travel she had wrapped a sheet over her saree. She might be on her way to a celebration, possibly a village wedding, but there was something unexplained about her, something in the way she walked. Indian women walk smoothly, straight ahead with a purposeful manner, but this woman sidled and stopped, pulled at her saree and peered through it.

In a waiting crowd the women flock together. As families come the husbands guide their wives and children to the group of women, settle them there on the floor and then go off to sit with the men. The women talk to each other and attend to their children. Here at the station a group had gathered, hearty village women, weathered and homespun. The woman in the pale yellow saree came near them but instead of joining the group she put down her bundle and leaned against a column. Suddenly with a little toss of her head, she let the sheet drop off her shoulders onto the ground and at the same time brushed the saree back from her face. She was a child, possibly twelve years old, a beautiful painted child – and suddenly I noticed that she had nothing on under the transparent yellow saree – a pathetic child with a thin undernourished child's body and a beautiful, painted, little face, provocatively artificial. She rearranged her saree with an elegant manner, using her small graceful hands so as to show their henna-painted palms. She flashed her eyes around the platform with a look of deep perception, picked up the sheet and in the most fastidious way wrapped herself in it. Then she walked slowly over to the group of women and sat down on the ground beside them. Somehow this unfortunate girl in her flimsy cloth, cheap tinsel and dustsheet had managed to create around her an atmosphere of rare beauty and adventure, even – it seems impossible looking back – even of exquisite refinement.

Hidden in the central hills of primeval India, seekers of truth began their search with a mystic prayer: 'the Teacher hath revealed from the shining horizon – the Immortal – the womb of the existent and the non-existent. Who desires knowledge to be creative? Poet, god, self-realized? What is the highest secret where everything becomes one form?'

Evening covered the station yard. Around the arc light circled a whirling cosmos of shining insects. They circled in wide, mad orbits like stars in the eye of God.

5
Calcutta and a Steel Town
1957

Calcutta, the largest city of India, the largest port, the outlet for tea, coal and iron, and jute products – this industrial giant on the Hooghly River at the mouths of the Ganges, was a good place to be, business-wise. Calcutta is an Indian city. As everyone knows in our age of so-called communication it is a city heartily disliked by most. By contrast, semi-Western Bombay, nearly as large, seems to be a world city. New Delhi, with all its then orderly virtues, seemed a transient place, a suburb without a city, as is often the case with new-town seats of government.

But in Calcutta you face reality squarely, or you leave in dismay. We were now and then reproached by American visitors: 'How can you bear to see the misery day after day?' – but the misery was there whether they stayed to see it or not, and I found their point less noble than it seemed at first. The poverty was an offense to them.

Calcutta – decaying, chaotically energized, the dirtiest and the poorest city in the world. Calcutta that was the seat of Empire and the focus of literature and of the arts, now is the place of those who follow after – of those who ride the whirlwind.

We moved for business reasons to Calcutta in 1957. Our seven Calcutta years were the full significant years of those twelve in South Asia. Our base was, as ever, in architecture, and it would be wrong to suppose that we would have been in India without it. But in our spirits and hearts, Emily and I saw that Calcutta was, over and above everything else, our home.

That joyous onrush of monsoons; the sinister noisy excitement of the *puja* season when the goddess Durga the terrible is worshipped; the breath of the sea at Howrah Bridge, microcosm of tragedies and triumphs; the River Hooghly with the mighty tidal bore surging up from the Bay of Bengal; the huge green trees of the Maidan, central park along the river, each grove a quiet retreat for the weary from noise of street and bazaar; the enormous bulls I respectfully circumambulated as they reclined at my office doorstep in the heart of the downtown. We tossed aside the doubtful virtue of objectivity early on in India.

Calcutta was a divided city socially: the Bengalis against the Marwari businessmen. The Bengalis of course had political control. The Marwaris, along with the British community, controlled the larger business contacts with the rest of India and with the world. The British, even then 10,000 in eastern India, were highly respected in business and welcomed by all Indians, though socially they kept very much to themselves. The labor force of the city was also divided: the incoming Bihari and the Oriya workmen opposed to the Bengalis. There was the debilitating pervasiveness of caste, and Hindu-Muslim frictions were heightened by the closeness to what was then East Pakistan, now Bangladesh.

Spread throughout the city was the great mass of Bengali clerks and small businessmen – the men and women who constituted its center of gravity and who also gave it its political instability. Strikes and protest processions were constant, were Communist-led and paid for. The state government was Congress in those days but for several years now has been Communist, and the city goes badly downhill today.

And so, our city had more than its share of hatreds, of failings and confusion. But its sorrows and its joys were greatly human, never reducible to abstractions – not even to the abstraction of poverty, for there is great wealth there also. But there are more *bustee* (slum) dwellers than in any other city. The rural poor at least have space and air around them. In Calcutta there is the desperation of total squalor.

Some of our Indian friends were connected with Calcutta University. Others had roots in the 'Bengal Renaissance' of the days of Rabindranath Tagore. These were the poets, scholars, lawyers, or members of the former ruling families. These and their parents and grandparents had made Bengal the cultural center of the sub-continent in the days of the British Raj. Calcutta was the capital of India, the second city of the Empire, before the transfer of Government to New Delhi in 1911. It was a proud city with a rich history, a city that had lived life to the full. Today its glory has faded while problems multiply. The films of Satyajit Roy, masterpieces of world cinema, are set in and around Calcutta and mirror the nostalgia of its decay.

A Palladian, sometimes Georgian, atmosphere, a provincial version of late English neo-classicism is still its architectural background. Large spaces, fine stairways, the all-important south-facing verandahs to catch the cooler evening breeze, perhaps a square pond close by. Often rich stucco designs fill the spandrels between arches, and exuberant floral patterns in cast iron form balcony and window grilles. There is usually no glass, but wood louvered shutters, adjustable against rain and sun – these buildings were well suited to the way of life of those early days – for the British understood and loved Bengal too. With their high ceilings and marble floors, these mansions are miscast as homes for the poverty stricken refugees from East Pakistan that swamped the city. There are prints by Daniels that show old Calcutta of the nineteenth centry. Its British neighborhoods were Georgian, and in those portrayals is the ring of truth. In them one sees the spacious beauty of that century – white colonnades against the green of trees in the open spaces along the river, with pavilions and promenades and bathing *ghats*. The English, released from their chilly island, gloried in this dangerous, expansive – and remunerative – land. Sometimes a note of ingenious fantasy crept in as when the bearer of an English agent won the sweepstakes lottery and built for himself a most astonishingly fine Mannerist house and garden.

We discovered in their neglect two Bengali temples to Laksmi, goddess of light and wealth, the city's finest Hindu architecture and there is the gorgeous old Park Street Cemetery desperately needing protection in its decay. There is the Victoria Memorial, large, centrally sited on the Maidan, an expensive though inconclusive glistening white marble centerpiece, housing among much else the expert watercolors of Fanny Eden, sister of Lord Auckland, Govenor General of India in the 1830s; and the Maidan itself, that spacious park which stretches more than two miles along the Hooghly River. It is over half a mile wide; the landward side is defined by Chowringhee Avenue. Planned with the usual

British skill, the Maidan is the lungs of Calcutta, breathing space for sports, music, meditation, military exercises, gardens, picnics, horse-racing – and on the Asian front of World War II, the fighter planes took off from its center for the dangerous hop over the hump. For us it was for walking, to see, in season, the unmowed, white-feathered grass, the progress of the northwesterly storms riding in, high in the white sky. And on the Maidan one saw the many-faceted Indian mind working its will on British splendor.

Neither Emily nor I had managed to speak an Indian language properly, but in Calcutta as opposed to Delhi, English was widely understood. In my office the staff except the office boys, for whom my hundred words sufficed, spoke English to me, and Bengali of course to each other. I told myself that the question of language, at least in the cities, did not matter; but in any case after a nine-hour day of concentrated work there was no room in my head for lessons. But for India at that time, the issue of the national language was hotly argued. It had been declared national policy to make Hindi the official language. There was strong opposition to this, principally in South India and Bengal where English, not Hindi, is the intercommunity link. Hindi is generally understood as a 'bazaar language' in most of India, but in sections that have rich languages and broad literature, particularly in Bengal and Tamilnadu, the imposition of Hindi has been seriously divisive.

A Bengali friend, at the height of the controversy, received a directive from the national Government in New Delhi written, for the first time, in Hindi (which even educated Bengalis do not fully understand) instead of English. He was infuriated, and wrote his superiors at the Capital that he had given their directive to his cook, and when the translation was finished he would reply to them in English.

The Hindustan Steel Corporation, an autonomous body of the Government of India asked our firm to design a new town. The rich iron ore deposits of northern Orissa were being opened up, and in addition to the new city of Rourkela to which we had contributed neighborhood and housing designs there was need for a smaller community at Barsua-Tensa at the future iron mines. This was in the mountain jungle about seventy miles to the southwest of Rourkela. Off I went; this time from New Delhi by train through the wide flat plains of north India.

Throughout the Ganges Valley the ploughing by buffalo and by bullock went on in spite of floods, and the water standing in the rice fields was patterned out with little dams between. White egrets and frequently enormous saurus cranes that stand over four feet high stood frozen in the ponds. The sun shone on the high white cumulus. I saw a large animal galloping away from the train, seemingly half horse and half bullock – a blue bull or nilgau. The farmers, the animals, and the birds live on friendly terms together. The Ganges Valley is level and thickly populated. But it was the sight of two turquoise blue roller jays performing their dance in the air that marked the journey. Like falling leaves they whirled round and round as they plummeted down, and then again flew up in the roller-coaster fashion that has given them their name. Their colors are the purest and most brilliant of blues and greens just touched with black and red. As they are larger than a crow it is a beautiful sight to see.

Near the then new Orissan steel towns are the hill country and the tribal people. In that wilderness there were tigers and elephants along with iron, coal, limestone, and manganese. At Rourkela an able young man fired with the enthusiasms of the new India, met me on behalf of Hindustan Steel. He would be dealing with this undertaking. He sent me off to the iron mines with jeep and driver and an engineer through a scrubby rough-hewn terrain without the lush green verdure that the West associates with the word 'jungle'. The jungle cock, progenitors of barnyard fowl, flew in gorgeous color, trailing a two or three foot tail. Iridescent turquoise butterflies, and the 'flame of the forest', an awkward tree with brilliant flame-like flowers in May, all these stood out from the dusty landscape.

These iron deposits consisted of one or two long, parallel ridges like all the others except that they are underlaid with a dark purple ore. From the tops of other ridges there were fine vistas, and there were level areas wide enough for building although the lower reaches became too steep. To avoid the squalid confusion of most mining towns the homes could be separated from the work by the natural topography. A ridge adjacent to the iron bearing ridges, but one itself devoid of ore, would be the obvious choice for the townsite. The ground reconnaissance was covered by a two days' walk. A tribesman joined us, dressed in a bow and arrow more or less, offering to protect us from the tigers. These small people are unacquainted with farming of even the most rudimentary kind. Although by the constitution of India they are citizens, over the ages they have never been brought into either Hindu or Muslim streams of culture. For this project one of the tribal villages would have to be moved. It was a major change for this man's group. His interest in our work was prompted by many motives. His village – six small huts – was named Tensa.

The government engineer accompanying me was weary, or perhaps bored with these days of climbing, and on the iron ridge just a week ago a wild elephant had attacked a survey party which had barely escaped with their lives. So I went it alone climbing up to where the land opened out onto a broad, essentially linear ground form which extended as far as the eye could see parallel to the ore deposits. Verification on aerial photos and investigation of water supply would clinch the matter, but this was almost certainly the site we needed.

The town was also to serve as a rest and holiday station, having a cooler climate than Rourkela's. Certain little swales and ravines suggested themselves as sites for pools, but the hilltop itself would be reserved as open space for the playfields of the school, and a similar crest looking off down the valleys would be reserved for the hospital. The lower and more centrally located parts were suited well for the shopping and community center. These foci could surround the hilltop park on three sides, leaving the cliffside open to the view. The homes would follow the contours and as the mines extended their operation northward the town would grow in the parallel northward direction also, but always with the deep valley between, keeping a half mile greenbelt separation. As with city planning elsewhere, the making of a hundred small, but right, choices makes for a good town plan.

My knowledge of the Public Works Department, the PWD, which deals with all government construction was already such that I sensed our work would be a struggle. In the name of the 'socialistic pattern' it attempts to maintain its monopolies of India's housing programs. The drawing-board approach is adopted: people were made for sewers (not sewers for people), the straight run is laid down, and the barracks (housing) follow automatically. But here at Tensa the lie of the land would confound the opposition because the fall of sewer lines must in any case adjust itself to the curved contours of the site. There was no other possibility than the informal groupings of homes that I required in any case.

Back in Rourkela all of this was agreed. We were off to a good start. With the Rourkela Sector designs we had overcome bureaucratic opposition to our freely designed neighborhoods; presumably at Barsna-Tensa we could do the same.

In remote areas, and this was certainly remote, architecture and planning began with such fundamentals as the making of bricks, locating sand and gravel deposits, the checking of timber supply in the forest and providing for its seasoning. Activity is dovetailed with the monsoon when work is often impossible. It must be dovetailed also with local agricultural labor which helps with construction on a seasonal basis. And the building of roads also took its priorities from available labor resources.

I checked the processes in use at the local brick kilns and described methods that would bring the quality up to a standard for permanent construction. The same for the seasoning of wood and the washing of gravel. Our estimates of building costs dealt with every such detail, and included schedules for the cutting and curing of timber over a period of two years. Quantity estimates for all aspects of the town were painstakingly built up along with designs and drawings – complete in every respect. And so work began in the field, the Public Works Department taking up construction where we left off with design and specification – the Karachi pattern that I had vowed never to be caught up with again. But here it was.

During these early stages Emily recalls that one night I raised myself bolt upright from the bed and, still asleep, announced loudly 'PWD', then went off to a sounder rest.

It became apparent that reasons would be invented by the bureaucrats to delay or destroy our good work. (The able young Rourkela man had returned to private enterprise in despair.) Our estimates for the cost of the houses were worked out with great care from first-hand research – plus experience. They came to

Rs. 17 per square foot. But we would never overcome the PWD contention that this cost was excessive. For them it would be a matter of protecting their monopoly of housing construction. At last, I asked the authorities if they would not like to withdraw from their contract with our firm and carry on in any way they saw fit. They were happy to do this, needless to say, and they willingly paid our bills.

When I revisited Tensa a year and a half later I saw completed houses only vaguely similar to the ones I had designed, but proudly posted by the PWD itself with the notice: 'This house was built at the cost of only Rs. 23 per square foot' – 35% more expensive than ours. But the more important fact was that the town was built according to my plan. On balance, the battle was about a draw but we decided once again not to be drawn into government controlled housing projects. Even so, the immense goodwill of India as a whole was to be reckoned with and remembered, and when I was invited to present a paper on this project at the Indian Institute of Town Planners meeting in 1962 in Bhopal, the government planners present, including members of the PWD, were, as far as I know, content with what I had to say about Tensa.

Design by bureaucratic control threatens to become more frequent everywhere. Studies in England had convinced me that the success of their New Towns program was due more to the phenomenal skill of the British people in solid democratic cooperation, than to what was their rather mild 'socialistic pattern'. The English could have built their New Towns under almost any system – or no system – because of their own high capabilities. But in England, in architecture, while controls had eliminated the worst offenses, they had also eliminated much outreaching creative endeavor. All of this brought conviction as I saw at first hand the workings of architecture and city planning: the spread of socialist bureaucracy, well-reasoned and well-intentioned though it often was, is not an answer. My pieces for the *Eastern Economist* in New Delhi and for the *Amrita Bazar Patrika* in Calcutta attempted answers.

There were first-rate men in the PWD in India. The ills of the system were not due to the quality of the men. Nor were they due to whatever corruption may have existed (we were not touched by this). They were due to the deliberate removal of a personal responsibility for complete comprehensive jobs of work taken as a whole, from first to last. They were due to the compartmentalizing of the different aspects of architecture so that no one man or no one group knew, nor ultimately cared to know, what was the final outcome of an undertaking. This destruction of the sense of responsibility is a pernicious thing — architecturally and spiritually — for it quickly undermines the potential of men to exist in fact as men. The fine tension between freedom and obligation is the mainspring of any individual and social action. When it runs down as it often does in bureaucracies, administrative procedures alone govern the work; and this makes nonsense of their very reason for being. Where this splendid tension is undercut for whatever superficially 'rational' or 'humane' cause, then, sooner or later, but necessarily and ultimately, there will be in the one case, if obligation is forgotten, chaos, or if freedom is forgotten there comes of course the tyranny of the State. Which way India? In any single case the reasoned argument, the side of the angels, is often with the bureaucrats, who can 'give' to the people from the tax resources of a central government. Yet the method of this giving can be a wicked one, destroying humanity, and setting the framework for a vastly reduced potential. One cannot imagine that the Hindu temples or the Gothic cathedrals were built by those who had anything less than passion for the final outcome. And this is the reason especially in India why the private sector of industry is much more capable of progress than the public sector. Job creation is not the controlling aim.

With commissions throughout South Asia I travelled usually by air, but when I had to go to a remote area such as Rourkela rail was the only way. Before the days of our driver, Laxman Singh, I took taxis across to Howrah Station when business called me out of town. The route to the bridge approach was circuitous, and at night the narrow streets were packed with all the varied life of the big city. Cars moved at a snail's pace through dimly lighted streets, and at this speed my driver, a Sikh, collided with a cow, which, as nearly as I could judge, sustained no permanent damage for it got to its feet again. But there was no chance for me to make amends. The driver, afraid for his life in this Hindu city where cows are sacred, raced the taxi through dark alleys to escape the anticipated fury of the passers-by, and I could only stop him with difficulty in some black, deserted, and unknown lane. Angry with his performance, I got down from the cab with my bedding roll and luggage, still hoping to catch my train to Orissa. A rickshaw helped for a while but traffic proved to be completely jammed on Howrah Bridge – not even the rickshaw could get through. There was just time if I ran with luggage the last half mile across the bridge to the station – which I did and caught the train.

In retrospect these words are externalities. What is the intangible that so permeated the rich variety of India that it took pre-eminence and bound us together with the Hindu world? It seems to me it was a tension that *productively* united two opposites, the caste system with all that it implies, and an instinctive intimacy between persons, a direct contact regardless of caste or station. There is in India no search for anonymity, no avoiding of the glance as one passes on the street, and every act of life is personal.

The caste system is the cause of much evil, and is disappearing. I do not write of what ought to be – but of what is, or was, by experience. But the knowledge that one's function is recognized in the wider circles of family or caste, or in the joint family group, or the religious community, Hindu, Muslim, or Christian, and that that function lies within the love and care of these communities of spirit, this knowledge cuts short unhealthy anonymity, the so-called 'alienation' of the West. The sweetness of one's faith in others and a gentle confidence in oneself was at the heart of Hinduism as we saw it then – and Hinduism was a way of life at least as much as it was a religion. Wicked inequalities of opportunity also belong to Hinduism. Yet, at the same time, its best aspects could appropriately bind, and yet separate, the persons of the Hindu world.

Some form of productive tension is necessary and natural to the human condition, or we sink to a less than human mass and a counting of impersonal noses. I maintain that humanity is safe as long as large numbers of people cannot be found doing the same thing at the same time in the same place. There is in this respect room for complete optimism with regard to India!

The problem of the beggars was always with one and especially so in Calcutta. There is hunger and misery as everyone knows, but we suspected eventually that much of the rather ostentatious Calcutta begging was in those days a put-up job. There was professional begging throughout the country but in Calcutta there were businesses that hire out cripples and children and indigent women with babes. It was a sordid, scandalous thing, and brought shame on the city – and it was thoroughly unpleasant as every casual visitor to India knows. Westerners are the usual fair game, best if just off the plane; but even after twelve years I, being 'European', was still a 'newcomer' to the beggars who congregate at fixed hours on the important crossroads of the city. Calcutta has lost world sympathy by permitting this degrading display of often self-imposed misery and vice. Here the West is surely right.

Or take again the matter of household service, a function that is proudly filled, and lovingly accepted when the world is at its best. Few Americans are equipped by experience or by psychology to accept a gift of service, or of duties which basically can never be repaid – no matter what the wages are. But acceptance can bind two souls together in a sign of harmony, an act of faith. I must add that, like every human institution, the matter of servants can be, and often is, exploited wrongly – on both sides.

In the villages of Bengal there was a warm and sure response across the language barrier, acts of hospitality and of interest in our European ways, traditional acts of brotherhood. How do I know? Was I not deceived? No; I know, and I was not deceived. The countryside was my restorative from the pressures of city business. I took its gifts. And in the city, in our early New Delhi days, when I rode a bicycle to work, I would return home during the rush hours against the stream of cyclists from the Secretariat. And I recall the joy and humility of the conviction that we passing strangers were not wholly unknown to each other. And one day while driving an arterial street, a small boy strode out from the walk in front of my car with hand and head held high, and in good humor indicated that he, a human being, had rights of way over a mere machine – and he crossed the street by agreement of all drivers. These are the ways in which India brings its love.

India! In America we were often asked, 'Was it good? Was it bad?' 'Did you like it?' One does not 'like' India; one loves it –

or perhaps one hates it. It turns out to be not a matter of reason.

Not long after coming to New Delhi Emily and I heard an electrifying performance of South Indian music under a *pandal*, a flat-topped, gaily colored tent. Taking our seats in the audience – coincidentally by Ravi Shankar, the great sitarist – I was for four hours enthralled with the controlled immediacy of a powerful duel between the vocalist and the tabla (an Indian drum) player. There was a unity of purpose between the two as they yielded and attacked. So unlike the harmonically prepared changes of Western music, Indian classical music uses a single mode, or raga scale throughout the piece, and selects within that raga certain sequences for emphasis. The raga includes what would be called in western terminology both concord and discord, and since there are no modulations these melodic sequences have direct impact.

This, my first real hearing, for which the sessions in London and in Turki were but preliminary, was a gigantic creation of mathematically and emotionally elaborated rhythm – much of it of lightning complexity – which showed our jazz rhythms, even at their best, to be crude and easy. Palgat Mani was at the tabla and Semengudi Srinivasi was the vocalist, and there was a tambura, a stringed instrument that provides the drone. There is no harmony in Indian music, if by that is meant the simultaneous sounding of tonally related notes – always excepting the repeated tonic or drone of the tambura. But the cumulative effect of the closely woven melody, improvised within the stern traditions of the raga form, constitute in effect a mentally retained 'harmony' at least as colorful and evocative as the chordal elements of Western music.

Often, as with that great master, Ustad Allauddin Khan, the delicacy and clarity of an immediate personal expression – always within this pre-established form, was heightened to a penetrating lyricism. He was in his eighties when we heard him play. Each note seemed formed from some mysterious quality of those preceding it, the complex rhythms carrying the melody forward as if it were the very breath and being of the performer. The music seemed inevitable.

For our Indian friends whose concentration and delight was

73

informed by knowledge – as ours at first was not – the excitement of the music was sometimes enhanced by performing skills of their own. The shake of the head, the measuring of the tempo by a final quiet gesture, the warming of the players and the personal give-and-take of the listeners were the social and personal parts of the event. But the music was supreme, and each hearer carried away with him his own analysis of its success or failure.

A performance of Indian music sets out to explore all the melodic possibilities of the scale within the form and rhythms appropriate to the chosen raga of seven notes. The limitation imposed by the rules of sequence and by the selection of the 'dominant' note are a part of its content, but its essence is emotional and personal. The player brings forth his exciting discoveries. He is striving with the form, but he is equipped with the knowledge and long training that alone make it possible, in any medium, for emotion to win the day.

There are, traditionally, certain ragas for each time of day or season, ragas denoting the attitude that each hour may evoke – though perhaps there is as much of poetry in this concept as there is of music. But the concept points to the rasa (the raga's emotional meaning) of the music with its play of consonance and dissonance in a way that is foreign to Western music. The melody, thus, is a search and a setting forth of relationships, and the rasa, or type of emotion spontaneously arising from it manifests a refinement and a strengthening of vital processes. Without notation, it is still rigorously governed by tradition. The resolution of the tension between freedom and form, carried forward by a miraculous rhythmic skill, makes classical Indian music one of the world's great creations.

After Emily had installed a remarkable piano in our Calcutta flat I went to work at the keyboard. The day often ended with a two-hour exploration of keyboard patterns and the invention of melody – freely and not within the Indian system. Then, when musical ideas had been discovered, the result would be taped. But there were those astounding times of relaxed concentration when the composition came fresh and without previous keyboard work.

In 1962 two programs of my music were broadcast on All India

Radio. The first was performed by a pianist. The second was a tape-recording of my own playing – music surely not Indian, but nevertheless of India. This was my introduction to the second program:

> the music breathes and its face changes quickly. There is an organic form that often includes, like the *alap* (an introductory search) of Indian music, the very act of discovery. The factors that go into it are both conscious and unconscious and largely the latter . . . There is usually the selection of a few notes, in the preparatory stages. In other words, limits are chosen – though these are on occasion over-reached in the event; but within them is adumbrated the selected musical landscape, until that landscape is comprehended – then the music happens.

This too was our Calcutta.

And composition with pencil, and in a thoroughly Western manner, continues to this day.

In the process of competing for the industrialists' rupee, my expert Indian engineer-partner and I saved him money in materials and time. We would have found ourselves producing refined architectural structures, even if we had not been so disposed because detail and concept came from necessity; vitality came logically from the laws of gravity and new technologies were used.

Nature works through structural geometry, as with the wing bones of birds, the space-filling forms of the infinitesimal radiolaria, the shells of eggs and of bivalves. Strict engineering structure follows the laws of behavior of given materials as they meet spatial needs. It is not to be falsified by tricks of imitation, interchanges of function or egocentric 'form-giving' self-expression. And Nature is always three-dimensional – that is the shape of reality.

By contrast, in my symbolic buildings 'virtual structure', or apparent structure, is at work.

I worked with requirements for climate protection, hot-wet or hot-dry, each with its very different need.* We provided for easy

* 'Tropical Climate Control Techniques', Architectural Record, August 1964.

75

maintenance, another special Indian problem. For our work in remote areas our engineering supervision expanded into full construction management, normally the contractor's role – this too contributed to design. Where materials are costly and labor is cheap, as is the case in India, economy lies in refined engineering calculations which contribute to elegance of design. Reinforced concrete thin-shell construction comes into its own and much of our work used it.

We almost never found ourselves selecting and combining pre-designed and pre-fabricated parts as so often is done in the West. We ourselves designed everything from beginning to end, and fit each process to Indian conditions. Ours was a wholly in-house process.

We designed factories for the production of paper, cement, fertilizer, calcium carbide, automobiles, cotton textiles, jute fiber, spun rayon, tea, fans, glass and plywood. We designed materials testing laboratories for steel products, machine shops, newspaper press buildings, offices, residential apartments, and university complexes, all on a major scale. It was a general practise, not specialized. Many commissions were comprehensive so that the entire planning layout and all of its buildings were included – for example the Gwalior Rayon Factory with its new town of Mavoor in Kerala. It was satisfying there to be able to achieve true homes for laboring families for costs as low as Rs. 3000 ($700) in durable construction, all from local materials such as laterite which is quarried in a soft condition and hardens on exposure to air.

And at the other end of the scale came my designs for Calcutta's Woodlands Apartments, the Minto Park Apartments, and the Aftab Gardens Apartments. The spatial ambiguity in the rooms of the latter two stems from the sub-tropical need for movable spaces defined by seasonal furnishings. On the other hand the Staff Apartments for the U.S. Embassy and house in Rangoon are planned for strict efficiency. Unhappily the U.S. State Department U.S.I.S. Building in New Delhi was forced by the client after departure into an unsympathetic mold.

And I made discoveries: the overall plan of the Times of India Press building in hot-dry New Delhi, designed in 1957 to face the merciless west sun, is in itself a gigantic louver-form. Then came the stepped reinforced concrete barrel shells with watertight louvers at Lipton's Tea in Calcutta's hot-wet climate. And there was the open stair above the roof silhouette designed in 1952 for the Karachi Polytechnic Institute. The rainwater run-off troughs for Calcutta's S.F.Products Co Ltd fan factory are integral with structural requirement and provide interior daylighting and ventilation of the hyperbolic paraboloid reinforced concrete shells.

The funneling of wind needed for cooling a hilltop house in hot-wet Kerala, functionally somewhat akin to the high chimney-like scoops on the old village houses of Hyderabad, Sind, was provided by a wing-like floor plan; and, as in early days, there need be today no mechanical cooling (except ceiling fan) with its attendant noise, unsightliness, cramping of space, and operating expense, if designs are well-conceived. Even the difficult south-west exposure can be protected from sun as at the Star Paper Mills, Saharanpur, by carefully calculated window projections in combined vertical and horizontal positions. The style of industrial design is fundamentally structural but these functional considerations provide its scale and detail.

In other situations such as at Utkal University at Bhuvanesvar, Orissa, the primitive construction method of the laborers' hand-basket was retained for highly refined reinforced concrete parabolic shell work over the auditorium – two inches thick at the crown, and the workmen were delighted with the elegance of the finished product they had helped to build.

And we also worked out the very demanding requirements for the natural ventilation of large window glass factories and of large calcium carbide plants. There *was* no mechanical ventilation available in those days. And so, twenty-five years ago – and without forcing a visual fashion as is done today -- there was environmental architecture, each a special case, establishing the finished appearance of the buildings and the group. Just as there has always been environmental architecture in centuries past.

Where does architecture leave off, and city or regional planning begin? And how does one discuss the intractable social and planning problems of Calcutta? There is one outstanding fact about Calcutta: unless dispersion is achieved the metropolitan areas will have 30,000,000 people by the end of the century. The city dominates the river for 200 miles; the port handled over 50% of India's foreign trade. River silting had become serious and new port facilities were being planned. But the city would still dominate eastern India.

Sometimes it was almost impossible to get through the streets to our office because of the crowds. In 1960 there were said to be 1,600,000 people living in 900,000 rooms, and in the streets. The unpalatable truth is that voluntary population controls and family planning are more important than any amount of city planning.

It was the young Bengalis that were affected most acutely by all of Calcutta's problems. There were few jobs for those with education, no jobs for those with no education. Only the highly educated were assured of positions. I became involved in the S.C.I., the international work camp movement founded by the Swiss Quaker, Pierre Ceresole in 1930 to help with earthquake and flood relief in Bihar. Its aims were to bring volunteers together to help communities in need, and to help bring understanding between peoples. There were four Indian centers: Calcutta, Madras, Bombay, and New Delhi. Activities usually took the form of organizing weekend camps, and sometimes more permanent projects. The needs are tremendous, far outstripping this very small scale help, but S.C.I. provided an initiative, one open to everyone, to give, and to take. Membership was open to all who believed that personal service can be expressed through manual work, voluntarily given. S.C.I. workers wanted to break down caste barriers, distrust between religious communities, feelings of defeat and hopelessness in the villages and in the slums, and to replace them not with more dependence on government, but with the building up among less fortunate fellow countrymen of self-assured constructive activity. Our members, all Indian except myself, set the pace by their own example, and by their own hands and sweat.

Our work renewed contact with the India I knew at Turki, the India of the villages, for our group often went out of the city on weekends to places where a road needed building or where there was some such other unskilled work, and where we had been asked to contribute our labor. It was our hope, only occasionally realized I fear, that we would inspire enthusiasm in village leaders so they would join us next time in doing manual labor they had never thought of doing before. There were songs, recitations, and good fellowship, and often the heat and the work meant happy exhaustion.

There are so many words in the world today that immediacy of direct physical labor on behalf of others seems to be all that can truly speak without further devaluation of truth – words have become so cheap. But nevertheless, out of these camps grew a real festival of words – our seminars for college students.

The average life in India had risen to thirty-five years. It was and is a nation of young people, and Calcutta with its huge University is a magnet for eastern India's youth. There were in those days 125,000 students in this University alone. All universities and colleges in the city were demoralized by the pressure of numbers and were politicized by the Communists. Therefore they grew less and less useful, teaching standards going down dramatically. The graduates had little hope of employment after graduation.

Communist agitators were continuously active inside the University and out. The most fantastic of all the agitations during our stay were the widespread student strikes in 1959, with mass exodus from examination halls when an examination was not to the students' liking.

The President of India spoke at that time: 'There is too much stress on rights in our country. Every section of the people is not anxious to claim but to enforce its rights, while in the midst of the resultant noise the call of duty is either forgotten or relegated to a position of insignificance.'

Students began to think of themselves as a class. Perceptive Indian statesmen were calling this a crisis of character, with its roots in the whole society. Young people want a place for achievement, discussion, and study, but attitudes and facilities were not there – nor were they for the most part available in the students' overcrowded homes. It was our effort in the seminars to point out the positive opportunites in the situation as it stood – even while recognizing all the wrong-headedness of over- centralized procedures, external university examiners, neglect of personal contact by faculties, and the exposure to unscrupulous young politicians both on the faculties and within what was,

79

theoretically at least, the student body. In the universities the idea of individual and social education had given place to the need to pass an examination in order to at least gain status, if not a job.

Who of the tens of thousands of students were these that attended our small sessions? I put this to one of our leaders, a professor of economics in Calcutta University. I was told they were by no means the most capable, for those were already in politics – and politics in this context meant Communism. Needless to say, we did not draw, nor did we wish to draw, those 'politicians'. We made the underlying assumption of democracy: not *whether* we shall have it, but *how* we shall have it.

But the temper of the time was shown by a young enthusiast who told me that India is the world's showpiece of democracy, and in another breath he stated that the minority must be 'annihilated' by the majority.

We did have good discussions. Indian friends, professors at the University, guided the seminars. The need was voiced for a new ideal, a new goal, to replace the rallying point of independence.

Alongside the baneful effects of cinema could be sensed a real hunger for the blessings of self-discipline. There was a determination not to submit to imposed judgements or arbitrary decisions –though there was a less lucid understanding of this arbitrariness when it was imposed by the Student Unions themselves. The view was widespread that a screening process for university entrants should be enforced so that undesirables could be weeded out at the start. Students were well aware that their own parents failed to take part in the educational process, so parent-teacher associations were frequently advocated. The appalling shortcomings and dishonesty in university administration were very rightly an object of attack.

One often thought, during the turmoil, of Gandhi's advocacy of basic education – practical education given in small and widely scattered schools and colleges, designed to make the student self-sufficient economically and morally. In Calcutta the great thing was to become a clerk, preferably in government service. It could not be doubted that, as in other ways, so in education effective Indian leadership had moved away from Mahatma Gandhi. Useless learning by rote was still the norm.

But the President continued to speak:

The plant of democracy, whether one looks upon it as indigenous or exotic, has nowhere grown without careful nurturing. The system that democracy has come to represent is the most complicated political fabric one can think of, which in respect of utility and durability is unrivalled . . . We believe in the individual as much as in the upholding of the rights of the society in which he lives . . . we want every individual to contribute to the building up of the rights of the State according to his or her ability, and, at the same time, that the State underwrite a suitable standard of living . . . For the achievement of these aims the democratic way is best suited.

Here in a nutshell is the riddle of the socialistic pattern that Mr Nehru hoped to establish. Add to the political problem the fact of India's population increase from 361 million in 1951 to 684 million in 1981 – an increase of 90% in thirty years – and we have the major elements of these next decades. In the seminars and work-camps we expected not so much to find answers in words as to prepare for answers by our deeds.

6

A Maharanee and a Maharaja
1959

Our friendship with the Maharaja and Maharanee Tagore (no relation of the poet) began with music, a tenuous thread from that first concert so long before in New Delhi – Ravi Shankar, and . . . now threads tied in and patterns were woven. We heard Ravi often in Delhi, had become friends and kept in touch when we came to Calcutta. Now, at the great festival season of Bengal, the Durga Puja – Worship of Goddess Durga – in hot, humid October, Ravi, now internationally famous for his classical performances, was invited to play at several homes. We were asked to dinner and music at the Bharat Ram's nephew's. Bharat and Sheila were friends and clients of Delhi days. Ben, out of town, I went alone. The Indian music-loving elite were there, no other Westerners as I recall. Since we would sit on the floor, I wore a saree.

After supper, before the music, an exquisite woman came in. Striking auburn hair, ivory skin, delicate and small. I remembered having seen her walk down the aisle of the theatre recently and wondered briefly if she could, with that coloring, be a friend's sister, whom I had never met. 'Who is that woman in the blue and silver saree, Ravi?' He looked over and jumped up. 'Come and meet her. I'm playing at her palace next week.'

I was thrilled when she asked if I would come to hear Ravi, and since Ben would still be away, Ravi would pick me up. This called for a new saree and the next day I bought a lovely white and gold with traces of turquoise.

The ten-day *pujas* were at their height that evening at the Tagore's. Each temple of the city had erected a huge glittering plaster tableau of the Goddess Durga destroying Evil. Bells, incense, flowers, a wild triumphant din attracted the excited crowds in an endless parade that surged from one display to the other. Streets were almost impassable. And Ravi was a celebrity. Jammed to suffocation in a tiny taxi, Ravi, two assistants and I in my new saree, tried to press through. The instant Ravi was recognized the pandemonium increased. Autograph books appeared in the car windows, hands to be shaken. The driver was in a fury, honking, swearing in Bengali; the mammoth Goddesses smiled down through incense smoke at this brash little taxi impudently nosing her worshippers.

Streaming with sweat we nudged into a narrow solid-packed lane. This is a great family festival, gifts are given, everyone wears his new best clothes, spotless white; children in the grip of parents jump and shriek with excitement. But some of the men, young coolies whose families are back at the village, become rowdy, and here, in the lane we hoped to navigate, wild-eyed men jostled the car. Ravi snapped an order at the driver who was clearly shaken by the whole ordeal. He leaned on the horn, stamped on the accelerator, we roared forward. Miraculously the people condensed against the side and we careened on to turn in between mighty pillars of a gate, a curved drive past rampant stone lions, to a doorway, open, massively carved.

A delegation that had almost despaired of us swept us up a grand staircase. Struggling to manage my saree I saw the steps. Dust, dirt! Bits of plaster, straw, dead cockroaches, steps with edges chipped. The balustrade carved, once white and gold, thick with a coating of grime and dampness, walls grey with stain, long jagged cracks and plaster pealing, panes missing from the mullioned windows, a faint smell of urine. At the top, radiant as an angel in pink and gold, the Maharanee. Massive jeweled serpents looked heavy enough to break her small wrists, diamonds like hazel nuts in her ears – the elegant scented mistress of that stairway.

Behind her stood in a grey silk shirt a man, stocky, grey-haired with wonderfully arched nose – the Maharaja. They ushered us through dingy curtains. Ah! *Here* was the Palace! The hall was a mere disguise, a mask of poverty to confound the crowds surging in the street beyond the open door. But behind the curtain . . .

The strange light with which I remember the scenes of that night! I could not have imagined then, seeing the magnificence, the taste, of those rooms, that it never again would be so . . . within months . . . And finally, after years of friendship when last I saw her the house had been stripped by foreclosures, and selling, and she in a plain cotton saree, her magnificent auburn hair in a thick braid that almost touched the floor, no jewels, was living in one dark room.

India had three kinds of Rajas: kings of ancient lineage, monarchs and rulers who were traditionally war chiefs and rulers of principalities; some reach back to ancient history and carry the names of kingdoms like Tripura, Udaipur, Bhopal, Indore, Mysore, Hyderabad and countless others; and then the later rulers, descendants of adventurers of five or six hundred years ago who gained states for themselves like Burdwan, Panna, and Chhatarpur.

Modern descendants of the ancient lines look down on the third kind of Raja – of the British Raj. Land-owning families appointed as tax collectors or *zamindari* by the British who in return for loyalty allowed them to claim as their own the villages in their tax district, greatly increased their lands, amassed great wealth, and were finally named 'Maharaja' for their diligence. Many of these men were leaders who wore the title well; the grandfather of our Raja was one of these. And he had been an exception among most of the honorary Rajas in having a brilliant, perceptive mind.

Building his palace and homes – they numbered more than ten – he modeled them on Europe's finest and filled them with porcelain from Sevres, Sceaux, Coalport, Meissen, from Ch'ien Lung, K'ang Hsi, Wan Li and Yuan. With tapestries; collector's furniture, a desk belonging to Napoleon I, a table of Chelsea porcelain; clocks – one called Four Seasons – porcelain figures four feet high supporting a huge ormolu timepiece, another clock from which small men emerged to strike the gong of time; paintings: Rubens, a superb Turner; rare manuscripts, first editions, signatures of the famous gathered in a library wing brightened by jade bowls, tear-vases, carved ambers and ivory – a sampling of the collector's world.

From the ante-room of the Napoleon desk Ravi and I were escorted into the formal Great Hall: a colonnade of white marble columns. And above a luxurious blood red carpet the ceiling blazed with crystal chandeliers and pedestal chandeliers ten feet tall branching to mammoth sparkling foliage of crystal – all reflected in walls of Venetian mirrors, some twenty feet high framed in massive baroque ormolu. A fleet of white and gold armchairs upholstered in red silk brocade floated on the glowing sea of crimson carpet. And sitting or strolling through all this splendor, the gorgeous sarees and brocade coats of the guests.

A singer was weaving his voice in the quick final notes of his raga. He finished, and Ravi settled himself with his drummer and tamboura player on the musician's mat. No matter how often I hear Ravi play, and *see* him, for with Ravi the seeing enhances the art of his performance, I am amazed at the transformation of man into artist. Taking up his sitar, grasping its narrow waist firmly; delicately, rapidly running his fingertips – the surprising Asian hand, its fingertips curled back as if to intensify, to stretch the greater sensitivity of the tips – running his fingers over the body of the instrument, loosening, tightening the polished ivory knobs to which the strings respond, fingering the three oriental pearls at the base that give the fine shining placement of pitch – as he approaches his music, Ravi is all lover.

Indian artists are lovers. They choose their art at the age of twelve and in a dedication ceremony give themselves to the God of their art. Then they belong to the God, and as, in India, the sensations and acts of love are a form of worship and the performance of an art is an act of worship, the two experiences are subtly entwined.

At the instant of my first Indian music, I felt it as my own music, of wind in trees or around rocks, or the wind on the upland sweep of Big Sur where the tall yucca blooms to a thousand ghostly voices, earth-echoes of the music of the spheres.

As I watched Ravi begin his raga – the long-cut hair breaking over his intense, in-seeing face, almost angelic, a dark-skinned virile angel of music – the Maharanee sat down beside me. 'Would you like to come with me and see the rest of the house?' It seemed rude to leave the performer, ruder to refuse the hostess. Perhaps she knew by fact or intuition that this was her swan song to splendor.

We strolled in the library, stood a moment under the painted coffered ceiling of the marble dining room, its long table that could seat fifty at a side – their two complete services for a hundred were one of solid silver, one of solid gold. Then up a second but well-kept stair lighted by rose crystal chandeliers, speaking in a low voice she led me toward what appeared to be a terrace wall, touched a concealed door that swung back. We stepped through into the – the place of women. 'Of course,' she laughed lightly, ' now there's only me.'

The air was rich with night-blooming jasmine vines and tubs of the almost overpowering Queen-of-Night. From the wide, sky-open terrace into a . . . room? a twenty by thirty foot bed. It was both. Openwork marble window screens, white and gold ceiling and over the whole floor a thick soft mattress covered with a silk flowered brocade and strewn with cushions. Piercing up through the center of the mattress a three-tiered marble fountain bubbled pleasantly. To one side a long white marble throne, vine-carved open back and sides – seat of the Maharaja, surveying the harem at ease around the fountain.

Back through the flowering terrace, the secret door, she glanced aside at me, 'I'd like to show you my moon terrace.' Hesitated, then apologetically, 'I'm afraid it's hard to get to. No one goes there but me.' I felt that there was something she wanted me to know. 'I'd love to go Ranee Sahib.' 'Oh, you must call me by my first name.'

Down a dark hall, out through a wall door – I drew back. 'Don't be afraid. The balcony is quite safe. I come alone here most nights.' On a rickety iron balcony three feet wide and eight long, open sides and bottom, we walked on air forty feet above a lane fiercely lit and seething with a shouting *puja* mob, like a slit opening into hell, crossed to a wide recessed roof-ledge. Another, set-back, roof was still above us. A garden of sorts had once been secreted on this ledge.

In the dim night we walked between the broken ghosts of marble benches, cast-iron urns overturned and spilling stalks of dead shrubs. City effluvia had settled thickly, blending grey forms into night. A steel stair had been fixed – perhaps for repairs – from the dead terrace to the roof above. I climbed after her, slowed by my struggles with the saree. She was already in possession of her secret.

It was a long roof, perhaps over the library, higher than other neighboring roofs, and unlit except by reflection from the sky. A thick parapet cut off most of the street noise. Bare. Nothing to sit on. A high, stark solitary place, rough as the rampart of a medieva' fortress. It was a strange scene filled with undetermined meaning: She fragile, exquisite, bejeweled, floated in this rudeness, a small shimmering fragment torn from a vanished age blowing among the roof tops.

Here she was apparently free from some burden in the house below, its weight suggested by the joy and release now in her face, the drift and gaiety in her movements. Free to be alone, perhaps only here, in a house filled with too many possessions and peopled for generations by 200 retainers – servants, aged relatives, and relatives of relatives.

She had come to this house a bride of nine years old. At puberty the marriage was completed. The Maharaja was some twenty years older than she, an age relationship considered the classical ideal. For the twenty-five years since then, she had prayed for a child. Made pilgrimages, fasted. Her religious afterlife and her husband's depended on this gift of progeny, of a son to her husband.

For Hindus an awesome punishment awaits a man who dies without a son. In funeral rites his soul must be released for the next stage of existence by an act of his son. Without this, the soul wanders indefinitely on earth. Until recent years famine and disease took such a toll that five sons were necessary to assure that one survived the father. The average age has risen in the last decade, a fact not understood by most Indians; but the desire for sons is unchecked.

Deeply religious, this was her tragedy. She did not mention it that night on her roof, but told me about her dogs, her painting, a rush of words and laughter quite unlike the calm of her below-roof life. Later I found what I had guessed on the roof, that she was a high-spirited woman repressed into the patterns of her caste. She was not supposed to be seen in public, or to go shopping. Suppliers came to her, brought boxes of sarees, jewels, whatever she needed. She kept the keys of the house, and sat every morning for two hours on the storeroom verandah, her spaniels playing around her, giving out the day's supplies to the household cooks and to their personal cook, reviewed the household accounts presented by the cold-eyed major domo.

An American's freedom, my freedom, appealed to her. Later, the two of us shopped in her little car driven by an ancient servant who could barely see the road. Ben and I accompanied her to hear classical music in private homes, often orthodox homes, inaccessible to foreigners. She was learning to take to modern ways and we would sometimes go to charity performances at theatres, to tennis matches, the winter dog shows where her spaniels were exhibited.

At our apartment a courteous inspection of our few possessions, our few rooms, and she would say how she would love to have a small quiet place away from the slums that had grown around them. She was afraid of the slum people. Someday she said, they would swarm up the stairs and take over the house. But the Raja's mother, an aged white-haired woman was with them. As long as she lived they could not leave the family shrine.

One evening the Maharaja asked us to supper at their river house. We drove out with them through the bullock carts and careening trucks, drove down crowded lanes to a high wall, entered the 1890s. A wrought-iron fantasy, a small square pagoda house, all curly grilles and terraces set in a garden that tapered to a fanciful pergola like a walk-in lantern perched on the high bank of the river. The cook had come early, and an exotic meal, planned with care by the Maharaja, of fish and spiced green mango and rice in coconut milk was served on the vine-covered verandah.

Naturally shy, the Maharaja in an expansive mood had a quixotic wit. He was a nephew of the former Raja, who being childless had adopted him. He had the dignity of his title but not, I think, an inclination for its responsibilities. Partition had taken the bulk of his land but he had still remained one of the wealthiest of the *zamindari*, the great landowners of Bengal. He was, when we met him, in the process of losing it all. We did not know of course that he was about to raise the money for a trip to the USA by mortgaging some of his last possessions – the contents of the palace we had seen.

One day the Ranee called on me. She had heard that new methods of conception had been developed in America. What did I know about them? At my suggestion she wrote friends then at home in Connecticut. On her behalf a gynaecologist in Boston was written and she apparently persuaded the Maharaja that they should go. In a glorious tour of America they hired Hertz cars, got lost on speedways; in Chicago a man thinking the fair-skinned Ranee was a Caucasian abused the dark-skinned Raja – they took it in their stride. But there was in the conclusion no offspring from the expensive trip.

Each year at Durga Puja we called on them, had tea in the ante-room and listened to the chanting, the bells and clamour coming from the inner court where annually the household gods were installed and the courtyard thrown open to the worship of the neighborhood. The appointments of the room were shrouded in cloth, and also the porcelain and the statues of the first gala evening. And each year another fine picture was gone from the walls, a lesser one in its place. 'Out to be cleaned, to have the frame repaired,' I was told when I asked where the Turner or the Rubens had gone.

On the first *puja* after their trip we were invited to join them for the evening of the final day. Now surely the Great Hall would be open. But our taxi was directed to a small side door where Ben and I separated; he was conducted away by a servant, while the Maharanee lead me into a small back room on the ground floor. As we went in she explained that women were not allowed at this ceremony. A number of women relatives sat on the floor, some playing cards, others leaned against cushions chatting lazily. She arranged cushions for me and I saw how women of the aristocracy often amused themselves. And another facet of her talent was shown to me, her music. I had discovered that her painting and drawings were forceful, exceptional. Now a servant brought her a guitar. Suddenly with a tense musicianly calm she launched into a classical *raga*, with power and technique. I felt a great love for this brilliantly talented gentle and submerged woman.

Apparently there was no turning back the collapse of fortunes. Every investment failed – bad advisors, some dishonest, and there was his own feeling of the momentum of downfall. Perhaps even an objective sense of its drama. We did not know the full state of affairs until much later.

We didn't hear from them for months, I called once or twice; she was out. Not long before I left India a set of chairs appeared in an auction house that resembled the Maharaja's chairs. In a few days the Ranee telephoned to ask me to come as soon as possible.

Led by a servant I went up the stairs. Big padlocks were on the ante-room doors, the Great Hall doors. Up past the library, padlocked. Down a dusty corridor to the old music room. A bed, table, three chairs and she herself. Almost more beautiful than before, in her unadorned state. She led me to a chair, sat across from me her hands clasped together. 'We're in terrible trouble. Everything is gone. They have foreclosed, there is nothing. Half the house is lost, the river house gone. They've taken everything. You must help me. I have only my jewels, my own jewels from my family when I came as a bride . . . If they know, they will take them too, and I will have nothing . . . Take them away for me. Sell them, hide them. If I can ever get away, I will have something.' 'Darling friend, I would do anything, but you yourself must come away and bring your jewels with you. Go to your brother's house. Anywhere, but don't stay here in this misery.' She was silent a long time. 'I want to go. I think sometimes that I must run away, but I know that I can never leave my husband. I belong to him. Whatever happens to him, I must share. I may be the cause. Only if I die can I be free. I will go to bed soon and not get up again.' 'You must stop that nonsense. You're a lovely young woman, half your life is ahead of you. Come with me, now! You can get a job, you can do anything you want.' 'I know I could. If only my husband would talk to me. I could help. I've managed this great house since I was sixteen. I can manage money. But the evil on my husband is because I have given him no son. Now I must stay with him to the end.' I agreed to talk to the jeweler about selling her jewels, but I could not, of course, take them, and that was the last time I saw her.

Months before this, the film director Satyajit Roy had begun the filming of an evocative tale called *Jalsagar*, a tale of the decline of a wealthy landowning family of north Bengal. He had borrowed hookahs, carpets, and most of his stage set from the Tagores and had built a replica of their marble hall, for they themselves epitomized his theme. They invited us to watch the filming. The parallels were clear, though unspoken; and though the downfall was perhaps inevitable in our time, a pervading pathos colored the day. We four watched the quiet direction of the film; our friends, sensitive to each shade and play of thought, were filled with memories.

Ben was designing a mountain-top house for the old Maharaja of Sikkim's daughter and we were invited to visit them in Gangtok for the week of the Buddhist New Year celebration.

Sikkim had for the moment a peculiar status with respect to India, independent in some ways, but its foreign affairs and military policy were strictly controlled from New Delhi, for its location is on the principal route across the Himalayas from China and Tibet to India. Sikkim's cultural and racial heritage is not Indian but is Tibetan, and Ben could not resist lightly teasing our Indian friends about India's 'wicked imperialism'. They were generally not amused. The Indian military in Sikkim, quite necessarily, was very much in evidence.

The New Year celebration was a matter of state, a social and political affair, as well as a religious occasion with an ancient history drawn from deep in the isolated fastnesses of Tibet. The Buddhism of Tibet and Sikkim is not the Buddhism of Burma and Ceylon. It has a demonology with Hindu elements intermixed that depends on colorful magic and folk superstition for surprise and impact. This is a far cry from the intellectual and somewhat negative effort to escape rebirth in Burma. It is both more positive, and less intellectually respectable.

We came the short two hundred miles from Calcutta by plane, taxi, loop-the-loop train, and jeep through the remarkable Teesta Valley, a landscape that must be similar to that which inspired the ancient south China paintings of the Taoists - cliffs and trees melting into mists, yet always showing the sensitive trace of human habitation. It was not a wilderness.

Our friend, Kula, met us at her father's door, the Maharaja's bungalow. We asked at once of course after the Maharaja's health. There stood near her a small and unassuming elderly gentleman in a grey wool robe – surely not the ruler of Sikkim. But it was; we had muffed the ceremony by failing to present the traditional white scarf we had brought with us. And he had disappeared. Realizing our embarrassment, Kula – whose formal name was Pemachoki – arranged to the amusement of all concerned a repeat performance, and before long we were ushered into the throne room where her father was seated on his throne in royal array. She prostrated herself three times before him in the traditional greeting, the somewhat dangerous

Sikkimese fashion of falling stiffly to the floor face down.

The Maharaja was most cordial. We had seen his own oil paintings at a special showing in Calcutta the year before. A large gallery filled with pictures of mountains could be dull, but each of his sang with fresh clarity and crispness, and the overall effect was to lift one up beyond the heights. Somewhere in each were one or two apparently private symbols, a small blue cube, or a red triangle or circle. On close inspection one could see that the painter had not mastered his technique professionally. But, conceptually, they were superb. We were pleased to be able to discuss these with him and he was ingenuously happy to see our interest. He was a sensitive man of the old culture.

The three day New Year ceremonies – the masked dances – were held on a high hilltop above Gangtok near the Maharaja's residence where the rather grim cubical Buddhist temple was placed. His special guests, and his daughter's, were seated near him while the dramatic dance in giant masks of deer, parrot, lion, tiger, and ghost told the story of the destruction of evil by the protective gods. There was a Byzantine quality of gorgeous austerity and stiffness about the dancers and their costumes, an art form from the Asian north, and not from southern lands.

In India, the electrifying drama of Kerala's Kathakali dance must surely have the highest voltage of any in the world, and its refined knife-edge of shifting sensitivities as the moments race by had kept us breathless. Kathakali's gorgeous discipline of artificiality abstracted the realities of this world, melted them in its flaming crucible, and gave them back as revelation.

Not so in Sikkim. The dances were long, and the art form was not pushed to the extremes of human possibility as with Kathakali. But the long Tibetan horn's deep moan, the slow drum beat, the magnificence of the stiff embroidered robes, the rightness in this high air of the slow turnings and rigid wheelings, the strange masks, the conviction of the performers, were new and wonderful to us. Some dancers were monks and some were selected each year from the educated families and trained by the monks for this occasion. They wove an ancient world about us, not Indian, but Himalayan, a universe of primeval forces, and the Maharaja sat small and intent, explaining the meanings of the dance.

During breathing spells tea in thin china bowls set in silver holders was served with melted yak butter, thick and steaming. Numerous Indian Army officers and the Maharaja's able Indian Diwan, or Prime Minister, mixed with the Sikkimese gentry. During one of these intermissions the Maharaja escorted Ben about the hill and quickly looked up into the sky, 'Did you see that? The red circle?' He had imagined the great god Shiva, Shiva the destroyer, in the sky. The mystery of the paintings was solved.

On the third day the other guests had drifted off and Ben had gone about his house design. The Maharaja and I were alone in the royal pavilion to see the dancers fight through the historic struggle. I had been sitting modestly a few rows behind him. Suddenly he turned round, asking me to sit beside him on the dais. I said what I so deeply felt about the marvel of the spectacle. But he sighed plaintively that though others might leave on this last day he, the Maharaja, had to stay. 'It is my duty,' he said.

The scale and scope of the dance, the mountain sound of the long Tibetan trumpets, and the strange strong music in the temple afterwards are landmarks for us. The princess's house did not go ahead. The Chinese invasion came and it was no longer appropriate to build.

There is high romance and there is stark reality in our century —beginnings and endings.

7
A Palace for a King
1961

King Mahindra of Nepal, whose attention had been drawn to the Tripitaka Library in Rangoon, invited me to design his new palace and government house in Kathmandu, the Narayanhiti. Emily would share in the interior furnishing. There was the tradition of the mighty Himalayas in slate and native marble, in carved wood and brass, in ornamental grilles and gilded finials, and the Palace was to be the first focus for the pride and culture of modern Nepal. I was warned that His Majesty would be a difficult client but he accepted enthusiastically my first drawings and the building was completed as designed. The other large buildings in Kathmandu, the palaces of the overthrown Rana regime, were Italianate in style. The building I would design would be a symbol by and for the people of Nepal. I make no apologies to those who think these expensive public symbols are out of place where people are in poverty. On the contrary, tangible rallying points are more than ever needed in new nations. And especially this is true in Nepal. Beautiful ancient Hindu-Buddhist temples (for in the Himalayas these two re-ligions are almost inextricably intermixed) are to be seen today throughout the country – the glory of Nepal. They invariably fit the site, and their splendid ornament is functional, integral to the form and structure. It is not something merely added to it. 'Less' is most certainly not 'more' – contrary to the dictum of the modernists.

The Palace with its high central throne room and its even higher temple spire to the right would be a recollection – about which might cohere visually once again a Nepali purpose – a will that is needed to solve today's long-term problems and to maintain independence from its two giant neighbors. The King's policies indeed already involved more common people in the national planing process than is usual in South Asia, partly, to be sure, because the bureaucracy is very weak.

The construction of the Royal Palace was completed some six years after our return to the United States. Inevitably, perhaps, landscape plans were modified, there were unfortunate changes in interior design, and the omission of exterior finish. But the building stands out clear. It is a 'brave' building, in the old sense of the word. Perhaps some day the outlying grounds on the far side can be recaptured as its necessary setting. The King has now established what is the principal avenue of new Kathmandu as a long axial approach to the Palace gates. Emily and I had left Asia before our interior designs could be put in hand and that work was done by others.

During this work, I was asked by the United States A.I.D. Mission (Aid to International Development) to design the buildings for the country-wide education program being developed for Nepal – and also some further buildings at Tribuwan University, campuses that are now complete. Working in the field with these devoted American educationalists was a fine experience.

The then new campuses were grouped in and around Kathmandu: a Technical Education Institute at Sanno Thimi with shops, machines, and agricultural facilities, classrooms and a text-book production center for writing and printing in Nepali the nation's first school books; and the Multipurpose Demonstration Secondary School; and at the University the College of Education and Normal School and a Demonstration Primary School. Back in the Himalayan foothills at Pokara – a twenty days' hike – is a pilot-project elementary school, worked out in the simplest possible way so that elements of the design can be re-used on other remote sites throughout the country. The materials native to Nepal are marble, stone, slate and sal wood – first cousin to teak, so some of these buildings were built in the name of economy with these fine materials.

The towns of Kathmandu Valley are sited in a most beautiful landscape. The valley was lush green in summer, yellow and red at harvest, buff in winter. Ranges of blue hills surround it and over them are thrust the breathtaking crowns of the range of the great snow-covered Himalaya peaks, revealed or concealed by the movements of clouds. The air is warm and fresh, the light soft, reflecting pinks and gentle yellows of the sky. This was the landscape Joaquim Wehrman, and East German who escaped to the West, paints with marvelous perception. Sadly, much has now changed. The cutting of timber has brought erosion, and the country's economic future is uncertain.

Ancient temples of hard-burned, highly polished dark red brick, magnificent, intricately carved wood window frame-screens, and dynamic metal castings, are the treasures of this valley. Will they be preserved? The buildings are still in use – old, small, inconvenient; modern Nepal may continue to tear them down.

Nepal was vital, lovely and astonishing – the old towns especially. But in the end, I knew no place as well as India. My visits to Nepal were brief, at the behest of His Majesty, and always memorable.

Architecture, then, if technically inspired in structure and socially inspired in function, is an expression of the spirit of the place in which the building will be. In more precise words – an expression of human geography and the mutuality between people and their land.

To discover, to realize in three-dimensional space the *genius loci*, is to have become immersed in a way of regarding life – a thoughtful reverence, a listening of all the faculties, a taut and rigorous empathy.

I found again and again that when thought for a building rises from an intuition of the earth and the light above it, that that urgent conviction is born which gives contact with reality – a contact that fashionable, academic, non-traditional 'originality' denies. My purposes were not always to be novel, but to be good. Words of the architectural process will always be unsuccessful: a building is ultimately a fact. For the magic of an art remains just what it was before the words came and after the words go – it is neither more nor less because of them.

Patrick Geddes and Lewis Mumford, the pioneer planner-philosophers, show that in the Middle Ages in Europe esthetics were always either religious or practical – this was true in ancient Asia also. Limits of this kind are the friends of architectural design today – if they were but recognized. No one aspect can be abstracted out – as is the current manner. To present the spirit of the place and of the people is the architects' opportunity. This in fact is the substance of architecture. Unfortunately there were no other architects, Indian or Western, who thought or worked this way while I was there.

In the cold northern countries the quality of needed interior spaces is the central reality, while often in hot lands the quality of exterior space becomes the architectural essence, in other words, landscape architecture.

The urgency, conviction, and passion from which the architect must work brings the synthesis that is called design. Much work today is simply the denial of all seriousness to architectural purpose and the exaltation of triviality, novelty for the sake of novelty. Architecture does not come in bits and pieces, nor is it likely to be suddenly new – though that is possible with new technologies. With the Royal Palace I saw the opportunity as a continuity, collectively for the people of Nepal. The huge building with its different functions is a royal village, designed by one architect.

Tradition and continuity tell us that (built on the constants of humanity) the reconciliation of past and present, and of structure and space, will enliven the functional requirement. They tell us of the *spiritual* function governing public or symbolic architecture. As with the Tripitaka Library, the Jallianwalabagh Memorial, the house for Mr and Mrs Bharat Ram in New Dehli, the Kala Mandir Theatre for the Birlas in Calcutta, their Industrial Museum at Pilani, Rajasthan, and with other of my designs, my purpose in Kathmandu was to feel *why* the ancient buildings were built as they were, to understand the past of the people who built them – and then to work freshly, letting the merely intellectual part of this knowledge go from the conscious mind. This is to place oneself within the continuity of the living and vital traditions of Asia.

India more than other places cannot be rationalized. The best of life, perhaps the worst, is there if looked for. Subtle energy of mind – and also gross superstition – is thrown against high philosophical abstraction. Tradition works within the energy of the complex. This, I think, is the hallmark of high civilization. In India the illiterate share it with the highly educated.

So each building was for a special case, the special situation, the special attitude shared with the client – I was not forcing a single personal style on these vastly different situations. Both past and present continuities were placed first, and from the conviction that the paradox of continuity *and* the special case is central to architectural design came my widely varying designs. I was fortunate in my clients, Hindu, Buddhist, Muslim, or Western – whether in the very different climates of hot-wet or hot-dry, and whether for programs that were public, domestic, industrial, educational, or business; and nearly all had ample budgets.

Architecture can maintain its continuities – whether those of geography, history, or culture – while always being alert to, in fact discovering, new technologies. It can help protect the vivid contrasts of this world from international fashion shows. Ideas may be new or old – but are they good? Establishing continuities is the role of architectural design in the last decades of this century and my book, *Architecture and the Spirit of the Place*, substantially written in 1951 and published in Calcutta in 1961, points to this.*

My designs of the Library at Utkal University, the Times of India Press Building in New Delhi, the Aftab Gardens Apartments in Calcutta, the Karachi Polytechnic Institute, and the Calcutta residence for Imperial Chemicals officers are among those buildings which, in their divergent ways, reached forward in the 1950s. And our industrial work was inventive and far ahead of its time in Asia.

*See Appendix

8

Calcutta Again

At Harrington Street the guest house servants took care of us, dear scrawny defeated Rafiq sans teeth, plump efficient Vaheed, the sweeper, Sukaram – Sweet Ram, and Martin, our lugubrious Christian cook whose home in a village near Dacca washed away each monsoon. They were riddled with faults but I loved them all, and tried hard to spoil them as useful servants. Paid doctor bills, bought clothes, helped Martin with his annual house rebuilding. And there was an itinerant carpenter named Kishtu.

Kishtu made and repaired things for all the neighborhood. He sanded down my bargains, made candlesticks and a cupboard for me. He was small and wiry, very dark-skinned, his thick wavy hair a halo of dark silver, and he had remarkable grey eyes. His face was lined, but he was beatiful. Solemn, proud-standing with a craftsman's dignity. Small angular arms and hands and beautiful feet brought into play in the work. I would watch him, pretending to supervise. He worked with delibera-tion, his intent intelligence withdrawn into the mystery of creating.

They come to Calcutta, these craftsmen, because their villages are destitute. They leave wives, children and old parents who will take care of the cow and the rice patch. There is no work for carpenters where no one has money to hire them. Some take the separation lightly but Kishtu worried about his family – his parents, wife, and son – sent every rupee to them, starving himself, I thought, he was so thin. Every year he would go back to the village at rice-harvest time, and return still darker from working in the sun but with slightly more flesh, an easier smile. When I needed him Kishtu would come within a day or two.

One record-breaking hot May day I sent for Kishtu, needing a base for our Kuan-Yin figure. Rafiq came to say that Kishtu had disappeared; hadn't been around for weeks. Carpenters and repair men have no shops or even addresses. When they're free they come by and chat with the servants.

A month later Rafiq told me that Kishtu was downstairs. When he came up I was horrified. His head was shaved, he was too thin to imagine, walked stiffly, face shrunk. But his expression kept me quiet. I explained about the carved base. He went off to the Bazaar, found a piece of seasoned teak and we got to work, 'We' – because this was to be art, a gently modelled modern form for the Kuan Yin to stand on. I marked the shape on the wood; Kishtu chiselled. He worked without a word. Hands strong and sure. Face rigid. After about two hours working together, I, kneeling near him on the floor marking, indicating depths of chisel and sanding, I said quietly, 'Kishtu, what has happened?' For ten minutes the rhythmic sanding of the wood. Then without looking up but in a soft voice from the core of earth. 'My son dead, Memsahib.' 'Kishtu.' 'Telegram. I go. No doctor my village. I go far, doctor not come, Memsahib.' 'Five years past other son die. This son had school. All years I work for he have school. Grow good. Not like me. Now he gone down. Many years past . . . Memsahib?' 'Our son . . . he gone down, many years past.' ' . . . It is Karma, Memsahib.' He went away again soon after that, and never returned at all.

The house at 4 Harrington Street was Georgian old-style Calcutta, built with others of the kind back from the street. It had been the German Legation before the capital was moved to New Delhi. There was the elaborate plastered-brick gateway at the sidewalk subsequently published in one of Desmond Doeg's sketch books. It had a steel embellishment high enough for an elephant to pass under. Inside the gate the servants lived in single-storied structures nestled against the high compound wall. From the carriage porch entrance the stairway swept up three floors to the several apartments, which one by one we occupied until we arrived at the large one at the top of the house. On the south side of the house, away from the street, was a wide lawn edged with a garden and huge flowering trees all around. Like all Calcutta houses the terraced roof was flat, with balustrades and cast iron spiral stair, all eminently usable for sunbathing, or for the cool of evening. This was our Calcutta home, except for our last year in the Woodlands flats in Alipore.

Rafiq and Vaheed were the 'Laurel and Hardy' team of bearers which Mrs Gaspar supplied to her tenants – lovable, honest and unpredictable – so much so that we soon took on Basilio Berrera as our Indian chargé d'affaires. Basilio spoke English well enough, being a Roman Catholic, a young and personable man whose wife had died and whose children stayed with the Fathers; he was head of his family of younger brothers. He was used to responsibilities and able to live serenely with them. Basilio became part of the family. His happy lilt 'Coming, Madam' is with us still. Then came Laxman Singh, our driver, a key man in any Indian household because there were no parking lots in India, and no place whatsoever to leave a car. A good driver will always produce the car at just the right time and place under all adverse circumstances imaginable. This was his professional skill and the secret of his trade. And Laxman was skilled indeed.

Bhomara was the last to join us, and became our second bearer when the chores of entertaining were too much for Basilio to handle alone. Bhomara was a sweeper, an outcast, whom we first had met in that connection. Though sweepers in India must never serve food, we asked him in our heedless American way to become our bearer and he seized with alacrity the chance to shed his caste. Probably our more caste-conscious guests were never the wiser, or perhaps they pitied and excused us. He was hard-working and competent, and the lack of poetry in his nature allowed us to fall back on him when Basilio's and Laxman's occasional flights of fancy made them unavailable. These three were part of our household and of our affections, for there is a personal chemistry and mutuality in the servant-employer relationship that must be discovered and protected if the household is to be a happy one; and there is the responsibility to care for servants in illness or disaster. So the bond is well-founded in practicalities.

A friend found us our sweeper, Bhomara, and urged us to take this man. His stature, tall as a Westerner and husky, worried me, he would seem so unlike the usual compact servant. And I felt that Bhomara had plenty of drive but no steering gear.

I had discovered this combination years before in Karachi when a handsome husky servant proved hopelessly inept. Ben had surmised that where people are undernourished as they grow up there could be lopsided development; some full wits and inadequate bodies, others, like this fellow, looked fine but had inadequate wits.

We learned to love Bhomara, his devotion was unshakable, and he gave full measure of everything he had. But I sometimes panicked at the thought that, unguided in an emergency, he would apply his strength and push his arm, so to speak, right through the dike and we'd all drown.

He had great dignity as befitted a strong man. A heavy cabinet to be moved, Basilio would sing out '*Bho*-mar-aw!', would give him a few terse instructions in their native Orissi tongue, the big one would take hold and the cabinet would sail across the floor to its new niche. After displays of prowess Bhomara looked solemnly at his bare feet while we shook our heads and commented in admiration. The head still down he would bend his eyes up with what would have been blushes if his skin had been lighter.

Basilio came to have special problems that centered around the heights of buildings – though there were other factors. On hot nights the servants slept out of doors in the compound to catch whatever breezes blow, but Basilio felt that his prestige as adviser to the group would suffer if he sought common comfort with loss of private dignity, so we suggested he sleep on the roof of the house. This lasted for two nights only. Our questions brought forth the fact that his colleagues had pointed out that demons were always ready to hurl unwary sleepers from a rooftop. Demons are to be recognized when they call your name three times, and Basilio thought he might have heard his called twice already. So he resigned himself to the penance of sleeping in his breathless little room. He was proud of his room, had hung a bright curtain at his small window, had bottles of water with philodendron plants growing on the window ledge. Kept aloof from the other servants as befitted his position.

One morning after breakfast when Ben had gone to the office, Basilio came with a strange expression on his face 'Madam, there's something wrong with my arm.' He held out a swollen arm with a black blotch on the inside just below the elbow, as if ink had spilled and run irregularly down it. It looked terrible. 'Good Heavens, what happened, Basilio?' 'Don't know, Madam. This morning sleeping, suddenly great pain there like knife. I roll on floor with pain. Now very bad pain all arm.' He was sweating and breathing hard. 'But why didn't you tell us at breakfast?' 'Want give Sahib breakfast, no trouble for you.' 'Basilio, could it be a spider bite?' 'Don't know, Madam, Rafiq say maybe so.'

I called Dr Solberg and sent Basilio there in a taxi. He came back with the arm wrapped still in pain. He had been so overawed with the Europeans in the elaborate waiting room, and with the slick nurse, that he hadn't told them about the sudden crippling moment in the morning. I suddenly thought of scorpions, from what I had heard – it was definitely a scorpion sting. The nurse was surprised when I called her with the diagnosis. Then they began proper treatment, a long series of antibiotics and bandages, it was a dreadful and dangerous wound. A friend gave me good advice. 'Never go to a European doctor for such things. Our Indian doctors have years of experience, they recognize what it is immediately, and have special Indian treatments for them. A few years ago my husband and I were at the fruit bazaar. I'd bought a box of oranges and turning away from the stand, looked down to see a scorpion just curling his tail into my foot. It was terrible! The pain! My husband carried me to the car and rushed me to a "hakim". He did something, I don't know what. Terrific relief, and in about ten days it was healed. Your doctors have to guess what it is, have to look it up, and the poison begins to work through.'

Poor Basilio. The scorpion had apparently dropped from the roof beam, luckily on his arm and not his face. He still carried the scar when we parted.

That was not long before we left India. But the breakdown in our rapport began several months before. I was at fault, and remember it with that deep ache left when, by your own carelessness, or anger or misjudgement, a rare irreplaceable thing shatters in your hand.

The problem of servants. India is so poor, so hungry that it is a miracle of moral strength that nearly everyone is honest. The temptations! And working for foreigners, itinerant foreigners usually, unimaginable bounty at the tip of their fingers. I had heard about the padding of accounts, 'pinching' as it is called and slowly, I fear, I took on a little of that disagreeable foreign suspiciousness, so unbecoming, and occasionally even a form of cynical amusement. Long before our idyll with Basilio, Ben would tell me that I was too suspicious. I knew I was spoiling him. Friends would say to be careful or I'd ruin a good servant. Ben would shake his head and say 'Well, if any servant can resist your generosity, it will be Basilio. I don't think he can be spoiled.'

He couldn't be spoiled, but his spirit could be broken.

We had with us a set of flat silver, antique, from Ben's family, and kept it in the safe for use at special dinners. After Basilio came and we had no outside help in the house, I kept it in a dining room drawer and used it more frequently.

The set was short of dessert spoons and I had six made by hand, fine heavy silver. I put them wrapped in their separate shop papers in the drawer, unwrapped them to show to Ben when he came home, then gave them to Basilio to wash and put with the rest. I went to admire the spoons again. There were only five. And then the scene built up to a search of the kitchen, the suspicion, the anger 'Unless you find it you will have to pay us for that spoon!' until Basilio stood sobbing, weaving, unable to hold himself erect, his hands clinging to his face, and suddenly I rushed to the store box and found the sixth spoon right there never unwrapped, never taken out nor given to him with the others. Over and over Basilio sobbed 'How did you believe – all the years, years . . . ' We tried to touch him, he drew away, a servant must not be touched by his master. We wanted him to sit with us but he couldn't accept such familiarity. We tried to say we didn't mean – that we thought – but we had in fact doubted him. It was never the same after that.

Ben's first ten-storied apartment building – Woodlands – was finished. I was thrilled with it. The arrangements of rooms informal and dramatic, the view of trees in the Alipore parks with a sweep of Calcutta from top floors and all the modern equipment undreamed of in Harrington Street. And then, although it was a syndicate and the apartments pre-owned, we were offered a choice flat in the building, a fateful bit of timing. For one of two things was about to happen to me, either I would have to move from 4 Harrington Street or I would lose my mind – pile driving and construction on an adjacent lot, and a huge air-conditioning plant at the U.S. Consulate next door, punishing the whole neighborhood in the unusually hot summer; and the commissioned book I was trying to get out about Delhi. Behind in my writing schedule, I had a queue of real estate agents waiting to show me new places. And then Woodlands. It was scandalously expensive and we turned it down.

That night the wind veered and the buffalo bawlings came in loud and clear. I awoke Ben. 'Ben, we've got to take that flat.' The tears did it. We got up, recalculated, and at 7 a.m. took the place.

But an expedition with the servants to show them the grandeur of our new home had unexpected repercussions. Bhomara, though so close to the farmlands and spirit and style, was mightily impressed. 'Good, Memsahib. Very nice. I like.' Basilio, the modern man, hands behind back, stood on one foot, grinding the other heel on the floor, and said a withdrawn nothing. 'Isn't it nice, Basilio?' He turned away. Well, this was a surprise.

He was a changed man. As close to unfriendly as it was in him to be. And gradually the immediate reasons became clear to us, though down deep I felt that the heart may have gone from our relationship after that terrible spoon. For Basilio the Woodlands world was an impersonal world. The servants' quarters were lined up along a neat supervised corridor, everybody checked in at the gate, visitors not allowed in the rooms, and he would have to share with Bhomara. Who would he be there? Another white-suited cipher in a cell where *everybody* had an electric light, a bed, a quilt, was inoculated on schedule, checked in and out, couldn't have a lock on the door, a weekly inspection of rooms by an English sahib, could not have family or child visit, nor friends. As a Christian, Basilio did not feel that living with Bhomara was an indignity – we dressed Bhomara in white and treated him as a bearer (which he was about to become in fact). But the old leadership was gone, the drama, the sanctuary in which his individuality had been fulfilled. Not consciously did Basilio know, but spontaneously, with intuitions that lie deeper than reason, and are the core of hope for a too systematized world.

The moving was pure heroics for all of us. The accretions of six years. The coolies trudging up and down those steps . . . we could have built a pyramid. Basilio outdid himself, saying few words, the expression of one digging his own grave. Everything taken over, arranged, the old place swept out. Ben and I and Bhomara stood admiring wonderful Woodlands. Where was Basilio? Gone. No word. For five days. Not a word. We tried to trace him, sent messages by his brother at Ben's office. Finally he came, said he had been ill from the strain of moving. We offered an increased wage. But he said 'No', and he left us. He was right. More power to you, Basilio!

But Bhomara flowered here, walked proudly to his room, in the corridor, a big step up. He even learned to cook after a fashion. Here there were no decisions or judgements necessary, just follow regulations. And I suppose we saved his life. An abcess developed in his throat. We sent him to a sahib's hospital and doctor. He was a sick man but pulled through. We saw in his eyes afterwards that Bhomara would have given his own life for us.

We still had our driver. The one who had said, 'Name, Laxman Singh. I am Rajput.' This is very high caste, Kshatriya, nobles, chiefs and warriors, from Rajasthan. To have a Rajput driver, when ruling families of India proudly claim to be Rajputs seemed romantic, his papers had been good and we'd hired him. Whatever his heredity, Laxman was certainly made of noble stuff. He was not only a good driver. This slight handsome man had poise and finesse rare in any walk of life. With education he could have been anything, and he knew the problem . . . 'My sons are get education, Madam. Two sons. In Benares with wife, my parents. Best school. Then they go up, up. My money for sons' education. The big education.' His uniform was always spotless even when Ben had to catch a daybreak flight and Laxman chose to sleep on our kitchen floor rather than take a chance on being late. In manners, and personal habit – he was a devout Hindu and vegetarian, kept the fasts, performed daily prayers – with his courage, and iron nerves, disciplined by nature, the Rajputs could be proud of him. His was an aristocratic state of mind. He along with Bhomara were with us to the end.

But our first six years in Calcutta centered around our apartment in the three-storied house at 4 Harrington Street. The owner, the manager, the bearers, the neighbors, and ourselves comprised an *opéra bouffe* whose cast of characters interacted far and wide. Meals were supplied to our dining room by Mrs Gaspar, a formidable Armenian woman, through her cook and bearers, Rafiq and Vaheed, and this meant constant liaison between ourselves and the working establishment.

From the first day, the life that we lived in the Calcutta of those days was a world apart from New Delhi. Delhi was shaped on angular lines, colored to match the dryness and dust, relieved by glints of water. Our days were indoor with pursuits of cool seclusion. No one walks in New Delhi, the distances discourage it and, except for the business center, there are no sidewalks.

Our Calcutta was close-knit, with sidewalks, central greensward, shopping districts, financial sections. Here we revelled in an atmosphere soft with abundant water, lavish greens, yellow, purple-browns against elaborate iron balconies and balustrades, intersected with trees. Our Calcutta was a lush forest, moss hung, decaying, choked with undergrowth. A city to enjoy as an Indian city – a place of people, meetings, and promenades – everyone in the thick of things.

In Calcutta within months, to Ben's amazement, I joined the American Women's Club, the National Indian Association of Women, the English Speaking Union, was a friend of the Asiatic Society, two Indian music circles, a poetry circle, the Indo-American Society, and persuaded Ben to join the (Indian and European) Calcutta Club. The air was lively with action, the yeasty Bengali air.

Everything was wrong with our 4 Harrington Street except for the house itself. Along with its contemporaries this house had proportion, the scale of elegance. When the Germans packed up in 1914 it fell for a song to the hands of a ready-cash merchant who succumbed to the heady fumes of possession by seducing his bearer's wife. The bearer put an end to him one night, in the bedroom where we now slept. His sons were soon bankrupt and the receivers leased the premises to two boarding-house keepers, an Anglo-Indian (Eurasian) and an Armenian. Armenians, scattered from the ancient Byzantine Empire – world citizens, countryless – lived by their wits throughout Asia. Calcutta has its share, attracted by fast-dropping values, and quick-money enterprises. Boarding-house keeping can be such a one. The husband of our landlady died before we came. She thrust out her chin and carried on. This was Mrs Gaspar. The complexities of her arrangements with the owner were a marvelous excuse for letting the place run down.

I would telephone Mrs Gaspar, 'There's a leak in the roof. Water is pouring all over our things.' 'Mrs Polk. You know it, my hands are tied. Owner will do nothing. What can I do?' 'But everything's being ruined. You've *got* to do something!' 'Mrs Polk! Be reasonable. Listen! I cannot do nothing I tell you. Go ahead. Move. I do nothing!' So we fixed the roof. We loved that wonderful house. If it fell to pieces no one else would care. We fixed the water tank, repaired windows, painted stairs, planted vines around the servants' quarters in the front courtyard, paid half the cost of doing our rooms. 'Mrs Polk. Why you do these things? Spend so much? What's it to you any way?' 'Because it's a beautiful house, Mrs Gaspar, we can't bear to see it destroyed.'

Ben and Mrs Gaspar were seldom on speaking terms. When they were, it would go something like this. 'Mrs Gaspar, there's garbage all over the courtyard. The bin lid won't stay on. The place is full of dogs and cats. Will you please get a new garbage bin?' 'Mr Polk. Why should I get new garbage bin? For those people below? Their cook does it. Throws garbage out the door. No, Mr Polk. No bin.' 'Mrs Gaspar, it is a disgrace to the neighborhood for you to allow this.' 'Mr Polk! Do not speak to me like that. I tell you the bin is okay. You act like I don't try my best for you.' And after the phone rang down: 'Mrs Gaspar! You're a slum-maker, that's what you are.'

I liked Mrs Gaspar. She was shaped like a sausage, had crinkly chestnut hair almost etched on her round head, crinkly eyes, big thick smile, strong teeth. She'd educated her two children, wangled them to America in hopes of a better life. She did what she had to do, and so did we. We were allies in a war on the rival boarding house whose backyard joined ours. Armenians too, but long enemies of Mrs G. They kept a herd of buffaloes and cows penned in a secret shed built against our back wall. Secret, because there was an ordinance that buffaloes could not be kept in the middle of town. But a small exchange of rupees may have fixed it, for there they were, making the night hideous with their bellowing, especially during calving season.

Calcutta
Late Christmas Eve 1957

Dearest Mother,

This is the night before Christmas! I'm sitting here in my nightgown writing about it by flashlight. I have finally caught the mouse! The other night I heard a mouse in the cupboard. Ben woke up and said. 'Do you hear that? There's a mouse in the cupboard!' And that meant *do something*.

Next morning I asked the bearers for a trap. Trap? What's that, said the bearers who loved all living things, though they knew very well about traps. I stood there waiting, soon they went to the community storeroom, tottered about on broken beds and bric-a-brac. They came up with a battered little box with slats at the ends and delicately festooned with spider's nests – a cage trap. It's the *dernier cri* of humanitarian traps, cozy solid wood all around with those dowled ends for ventilation. The mouse shuts himself in by nibbling on a piece of bread attached to the wire that triggers the door. And there seem to be ways of getting out. The bearer whipped the dishcloth off his shoulder, dusted out the trap and handed it to me. I garnished it with bread and settled it on a plate in the cupboard.

That night, the third before Christmas we went to bed, to sleep, perchance to . . . Bang! Voice from other bed 'Got it!' Voice from mine 'I'll put it out for the sweeper.' I didn't add 'To kill' because I like mice and carrying the trap out to the hall I was sorry to think of killing it. And so next morning I saw the sweeper peacefully redistributing the dust of the floor. 'Good morning, Sukaram, did you get rid of the mouse?' 'Yes, Madam, I let it out in the storeroom where it lives.'

Second night before Christmas. Ben working on projects more or less around the clock: 'Listen dear, you've got to do something about the mouse!' He pushes his earplugs deeper as it's the season for nightly catterwauling from the garden. I apply the tidbit to the wire, turn out the lights, wait to hear the soft bang of capture, and carry the trap to the hall, confident that a new understanding now possessed the sweeper. Morning: I step into the hall to be met by a battalion of servants. The trap is suspended in the Head Bearer's reluctant fingers. 'Madam, there was no mouse in the trap.' 'You've let it out again!' 'No, Madam. No mouse.' And now *I* am trapped, and think I CANNOT ASK OF THEM WHAT I WOULD NOT DO MYSELF. But Ben describes a larger issue. 'Don't you realize that mice are disease carriers? and Calcutta mice . . . That mouse must be killed!' 'Yes, but what can I do?' 'Do? why, when you hear it snap we drop the trap in a tub of water!' And this was CHRISTMAS eve.

While Ben got ready for bed I sat there and just looked at the trap. Did that mouse really get out by itself? I picked it up and jiggled the door. Tight enough. Jiggled the dowels at the other end. Aha! One was loose, and by pushing it a bit it left a gap that a small body could wiggle through! Why that clever mouse. I could see it all now. In the storeroom the mouse might have been living in the trap. He knew all about it. But an ultimatum had been given. I hung the bait and went to bed.

Ben slept. I lay watching the moonlight brighten the leaves of our plants through the open door of our balcony. All through the house not a creature was stirring except for that mouse carousing in the cupboard. Then! The trap door! I was out of bed and over there! At last I knew what to do. Like the bearers I could never, never drown that mouse, but I could drop it out of the trap into the garden two flights below.

Stealthily, so Ben wouldn't wake and force my hand, I slid out through the balcony door, the mouse balancing back and forth in the trap. I can see it through the bars, fluffy, soft, and round. I lean over the rail, press open the door, and holding it out in the air give the box a shake. Nothing drops out. Shake again. Nothing. And I look in through the end bars right into the eyes of that beautiful mouse. She is clinging to the bottom of the cage for dear life. She looks right through me. Brilliant shining eyes full of living, and a kind of exultation of excitement as if she knew the Will of the Eternal Mouse and gloried in that testament, knew she had brains and religion on her side. There I was, face to face with her special gifts, encountering a mouse so superior that she seemed bigger than I, I more shaken than she. Now I can see that the last few nights were campaigns of wit, resourcefulness, sense of humour, daring confidence in collecting those offerings so suitably her due . . . if ever there was a Mouse with the Most . . . but to save her I had to shake her out.

I gave two mighty shakes before I saw a small ball fall out. I looked quickly down and as I look I see that directly, DIRECTLY below is the big rangy black garden cat, hunting, and as I look I see the cat make a startled pounce, right up into the air and OH . . . MOUSE BEAUTIFUL BEAUTIFUL MOUSE . . . Christmas! For the big black cat.

I had soon found the Calcutta auction houses. No more those plain plank tables, plank divans and cane chairs. A beautiful hand-shaped antique table. All line and proportion. Painted black, but it came back from the refinishers sanded down to lustrous amber Burma teak. 'It that a set of Meissen? Are those cups real Capo di Monte, or German copies, there on that old square piano? How much is the piano, Miss Mara?' 'One seventy-five, Mrs Polk.' 'I'll give you one fifty.' 'Have to ask the owner.' 'Well, send it over to my place, and I'll consider it while you ask.'

Fourteen small men – ants conducting a beetle to the nest – carry the piano down the street, up the eighty-three steps to our flat. The pain of their work! Gasping . . . three steps. Rest. Again . . . The coolies are so thin. There's always an old man among the young and very young, who comes to share the wage but whose shoulder is an inch below the load. Indians share with their aged. And the piano! It seemed to make the tone of two instruments, harpsichord treble, cello base, soft action, brought to Calcutta in 1865.

And in the broad shadowy room our huge plants, purple raw-silk couches, black-green and sun-yellow cushions, the grey marble floor, the rare piano. Of our Delhi things we had brought only our Chinese porcelain. On tables here and there, near plants and pieces of bronze, the three Kwan-Yin, goddesses of mercy, stood, each engaged in gracing her part of the room.

The USIS Cultural Affairs Officer then was John Stumpf; his wife, Karen. In a crowd – a party or meeting – when the going was loud and thick, Karen stood out for an imperturbable gentleness that seemed quite radiant. Her father an architect, her mother a writer, she had quick appreciation for qualities of art in what ever condition they were found. Driving with Karen into our rundown courtyard I complained to her that it was my despair. She looked with delight at the tangle of children, cats, laundry, plants, repair shops, bare-chested loungers, 'I think it's fine this way. Our place is so slick and American we could as well be back home in Minnesota. You have a wonderful village right in the front yard. Everything drooping and picturesque . . .'

John was as sympathetic to India as she, and Indians sensed it. After they were transferred we were often asked about the Stumpfs. 'They were tops. They had a feeling for India. They didn't want to remodel us on US lines. If they always sent people like that here . . .'

At Karen and John's we met writers, painters, poets – the milieu most interesting to me – and discovered the tremendous artistic vitality of Bengal. The name Tagore took on flesh as I saw Bengali life reflecting some lineament of his thought. Rabindranath was the product and prophet of Bengal in poetry, drama, music, painting, prose, and also in his concept of an academic atmosphere shown at his remarkable school, Shantiniketan, 'World University', and in his sense of architecture and land-scape. His genius had been stimulated by an earlier religious movement – the Brahmo Samaj.

In the 1800s a Bengali, Raja Ram Mohan Roy, educated in England, had hoped to lead India almost single-handedly to the modern age. Under Christian influence he reshaped a Hinduism that taught one God and rejected all images for worship or ritual. He campaigned for abolition of caste, equality of women, universal education – the gamut of enlightened social reform. He laid down political patterns that would free India from English rule, a freedom that was his strongest passion, and an inspiration, later, to Gandhi.

An English woman, continuing his efforts, founded the National Indian Association of Women, the oldest intercommunity women's organization. Toward the end of his life Roy founded the Brahmo Samaj, based on the worship of One God in a synthesis of the Christian humanitarian principles of love with the Hindu philosophical abstractions on the nature of Divinity.

The father of Rabindranath Tagore became the leader of the Brahmo Church. And although the Church has had a variable history, many of the important men of modern Bengal have been formed by its teachings.

To understand Bengal, the movements and causes, holy and unholy, the people, the arts, you must conjure up the near-tropical hot-wet climate. Stimulating and enervating at once. The thermometer rises to a bland 90°F. and you think you'll melt, perspiration doesn't dry in the water-filled air. Exhausted, desperate, then a sound in the trees, and suddenly the late afternoon wind strikes you. Wonderful, fresh, sweeping in from the ocean forty miles away. The air is luminous with ocean mist, the light fading to a silver pink glow. One drove to the river, parked the car, and strolled on the embankment looking down through the dust into little country boats where men were cooking over small fires under the cane-arched roof. The river water, brown with silt, turned bright like mercury stained with coral. Shadows in the water were lavender, ships and docks lavender. The freighters rode at anchor full lit like great orange lanterns in the orchid dusk.

Calcutta had then an atmosphere of mystery, of the juxtaposing of anomalies and suspended reality. An early morning ground-mist would lie over the acres of the Maidan, shrouding trees, making it pale, bright, obscure. Pockets of fog thicken, clear, deepen again around separated white-clad figures – early risers – fixed on the silvery grass in the various positions of yogic exercise. The white fog swirled off to reveal perhaps a dark bat-like shadow that became the bronze statue of a rearing horse, with a British General in his fog-blackened cape.

I had been on the Executive Committee of the National Indian Association of Women which had a multi-national membership for two years when I was asked to be President. I was amazed. I was the dark horse.

When the Committee approached me I made a condition: if they, the key women of the Club, would support my proposed redirection with less emphasis on tea parties, I would be interested. 'Yes, yes, we will all support it.' And I entered my Presidency with enthusiasm. I gave a somewhat grandiose inaugural address, and worked out a reform crash program –

even now it seems quite ingenious – selected my leaders, and we were off. Then the Chinese armies invaded India.

Calcutta, jet-minutes from Tibet, had the tension of a frontier post. Dropping everything we arranged first-aid classes, soldier's aid committees, knitted, flung our energies about with useless abandon, to the tolerant amusement of the harassed Military High Command who asked us please not to send any more packages of tea and cigarettes for the forward troops, for they could get them over the passes only by plane and there were none to spare.

All the women's clubs I knew were doing the same things, charm and vigor at full tide. Her Excellency Padmaja Naidu, Governor of West Bengal, called a city-wide meeting. Hundreds of women crowded into a conference room at the Governor's Mansion, leaders of hard working welfare groups. As the Indian women, excited by the occasion and proud of their work, jumped up to tell what their groups had done, I felt that our efforts were very humble, and until Her Excellency called on me, I held back, a reluctance with two effects, the personal prestige of being called by name, and the slight annoyance of my committee because I had not been on my feet with the rest of them. But at that time of national soul-searching, the initiative and discipline had to be Indian; it seemed awkward to be sufficiently aggressive and yet a *foreign* president of an essentially Indian organization. I loved the women of the NIA, enjoyed their wonderful friendliness, respected them, but was glad when my term ended. I was already pondering another book project.

We met the Keyserlings one day. The Keyserlings were astrologers, numerologists and philosophers. Their small run-down garden-house stood in a bare ruined garden with crumbling walls. Tacked on their sagging front door was their card 'Count and Countess von Keyserling.'

Arnold is Bismarck's great-grandson and Willi is a princess of the ancient Austrian house of Auersperg. Arnold's father, the philosopher and Asian traveller, had been close to Rabindranath Tagore, and Arnold and Willi had just completed a teaching assignment at Santiniketan, Tagore's school. They'd lived in Egypt, and Venice and Positano and in Paris. Willi had been a principal cutter for Dior, the Parisian dress designer, after World War II had changed her circumstances.

In February, a multifaceted astronomical event took place that occurs but once in about twenty-five thousand years – this much is fact whatever one makes of it. Arnold as well as all the astrologers of India and Nepal made a great deal of it. Some four epochs of cosmic cycles come to an end at that moment and others begin. We were invited to breakfast at 4.24 a.m. – the exact moment of our passage to the new Age. Arnold, a philosopher of standing, gave us an erudite exposition of the meaning of the new Age and of the differences between that of the Fish and that of the Water Carrier. As I suspected it would not be one to our liking; its hallmark would be the group, rather than the individual.

The timing was suitably mystic – at the stroke of the moment Willi lit the paper under a huge bonfire they'd built, the flames shot up into the still night sky. We could hear wild drumming from the city's temples and a ghostly pulse in Arnold's prophecies as he stood reading in the firelight.

9
Orissa

The hotel at Puri in the state of Orissa stands on a beach in the Bay of Bengal. It is thick with generations of paint and striped by long shaded verandahs behind a low compound wall. The same decrepit car that had brought us from the station to the hotel would soon take us to Bhuvaneswar, the capital of the state of Orissa. Ben had discovered that it was the only car available in town and the driver was reliable. We rattled away. At the petrol station I was struck by the listlessness of the people. They were friendly and clean, but slow-eyed, their thought processes apparently working at quarter speed. We had read that Orissa was a backward area, and the men we had seen idling around the station and along the streets, plus a certain enervated atmosphere in the town, confirmed it.

Orissa. What could be done to begin the return to her ancient glory. She had been called the great kingdom of Kalinga; in the third century B.C. Emperor Ashoka reached out to conquer her. Long after that Kalinga maintained her greatness. She became known as Orissa, and supported mighty kings who built majestic temples. The last north Indian kingdom successfully to resist the Muslims, she was not conquered until the sixteenth century. The kingdoms of Ancient India lived by the sword, now India lives by ploughshares . . . but could the man at the filling station be a son of heroes?

On the road to Bhuvaneswar we passed country carts and groups of villagers. Farmers worked in the rice fields. Here were the country people. We passed a young farmer on his bullock cart. He sat leaning forward, elbow on knee, swinging his foot, the rope loose in his hand. A cotton shawl he had worn during the earlier chilly morning was thrown back and the sun made his skin shine. The flesh of his body and arms was firm and lively over full muscles. When he turned around to watch us overtake him, I saw that he had quick eyes and a mouth ready to smile.

Entering a village the people were buoyant and healthy, neither fat nor thin, and the beaming naked children who ran to watch us go by were growing into handsome adults.

'Look at these country people! Aren't they fine after that decrepit town crowd?'

'That's what Vinoba Bhave tells India. He says the villagers will be the ones to rebuild India.'

'These really *are* sons of Kalinga. You can see the old strength in them.'

The villages we were seeing were spotlessly clean, not a fly in the air. No litter or broken houses or untidy rags. No vulgar cinema advertisements on the walls, no beggars, no nervous self-abused idlers, none of the town sights. Some of the tribal Santal villages were away from the road with paths or narrow roadways that branched from the highway and led through a graceful jungle of coconut palms, bamboo groves – lighted by filtered sun from within like a cluster of haloes – guava trees, and mangoes. Huge pipal trees stood on either side of the road, the whole countryside a delightful creation of tree-made spaces.

The houses were of earth, coatings of soft mud smoothed plastically over the walls and floors and steps until they merged with rounded edges into one undulating pale café-au-lait surface. It is a finish used in many parts of India, that dries hard and can be swept for a long time before being redone. On the outside walls, especially around the doors, the women had painted intricate designs in white rice flour, exquisite and innocent like white lace on fawn-colored velvet. Add the dark brilliant blue, the special fabric color of the area. Sarees are blue, shirts are blue; a blue saree is hung to dry over the porch rafter of a lace-painted earthen house, and add the luminous jungle greens.

The road moved through refreshing and quiet variations. First jungle, then villages, then open land in rectangular fields stretching to the near horizon of trees. These rice paddys had recently been replanted so that a flush of new green spread between the raised paths that divided them. Farmers repairing the low embankments in anticipation of the summer flooding of the fields stood up to watch us pass. White herons balanced on one red leg in the pale green sprouts. There were hunched paddy birds, grey and invisible until they flew, then brilliant white; a type of bittern on embankments of grass, remarkably camouflaged with green stripes, a transparent bird; and at one place three great white cranes spread their grey-bordered black-edged wings and flew slowly to a safe distance trailing their red legs over the young green rice.

We came to fields where water lay in shallow pools – kingfishers brown and white when sitting – but dark bright blue – the saree blue – in flight, and the long red bill. The astonishing music of Indian rural colors played together.

We looked far across the flat land which was part of the wide border of the Bay of Bengal and the driver solemnly pointed to a tall tree-banked silhouette on the skyline.

Then, 'Lingaraj!'

On a low rise of land – probably the rubble of the ancient capital of the Kalinga Kings – the old town of Bhuvaneswar clusters around this impressive temple. We drove slowly through the narrow streets and, turning a corner, the temple towered ahead of us. A tall gate and high wall enclosed it and a crowd of people were milling around the gate.

I pulled a scarf over my head and put my hand on the door. We had come more than a thousand miles from Delhi to see this temple; it had come a thousand years of time to welcome us. When we got down a crowd of shouting 'guides' blocked our way.

'No guides, no guides,' we said sternly. 'Absolutely no!'

'Absolutely no!' the guides mocked.

We walked quickly towards the closed gate followed by the crowd. A platform had been built with a stairway up one side. We hurried up the steps hoping to shake them off. They clambered after us.

From there we could see the courtyard with its group of small temples and the great Lingaraj.

A boy leaned over the rail and pointed to the temple.

'That Lingaraj temple.'

'No guide,' we said. Then, although reluctant to ask the boy anything, 'We want to go in. Where do we go in?'

'You not in,' the boy said. 'You not Hindu.'

We stood astonished. Not in, after the long long journey, and the jostling dusty three-hour ride.

There would be no discovery from a loveless platform. No discovery while peering like hurried tourists over a wall. 'Have a look, lady, have a little look at the nice old temple.'

I suddenly felt angry and cheated, turned abruptly and went down the stairs. In the car I leaned against the cushion.

'Let's go on.'

'I want to see more of it.'

'Yes, but let's get away from this place.'

The driver started the engine. The guides gathered around the car and the boy who had pointed at the temple put out his hand and demanded four rupees. We ignored him. Then a young man with long smooth hair and spotlessly white clothes came to the window of the car.

'This boy talked to you up there – you owe him two rupees.'

We stared at him. 'Ridiculous, we owe him nothing.'

'Alright, then,' said the man, 'one rupee. You must give him one rupee.' We held our hands out to the man. 'You give us one rupee. Come on, one rupee. You give us one rupee.'

The guides were struck silent. The man looked at us sitting there with our hand stretched out and then began to laugh. Everyone laughed. It was a wonderful joke. We drove away.

At the next block we told the driver to stop. We were at the back corner of the temple wall. It was quiet, no crowds here. I stayed alone in the car. The driver got out and sat down across the road.

The temple was on the left and to the right shops curved along the slope of the land. People laden from market or just strolling in the sunshine. They glanced at me but did not stop or stare and it was pleasant to sit quietly there and watch the town life; an old man with flowers in his hand, friends that stopped to talk, three women who carried baskets on their heads.

Across the road a wide flight of steps led up to a small house divided into two sections, a living quarter and a shop. In front of it, the proprietor strolled back and forth with his infant son on his hip. He was an energetic young fellow with not enough physical work to do, so he kissed his baby, scratched his head and idled restlessly in the sun while he waited for customers.

A boy ran up the hill dexterously rolling a bicycle-rim hoop. As it whirled near, the proprietor snatched it, then took the stick from the boy's hand and, running with the infant abounce on his hip, rolled the hoop wildly in all directions. Finally he gave it a mighty shove, threw the stick after it, and laughed as the boy chased down the road.

Four well-fed russet chickens enjoyed the delicacies of the road near where the proprietor sauntered, a large masterful cock, two charming hens, and a tall awkward adolescent cock with his comb and wattles just beginning to fill. They all pecked away happily until the master cock finding the larger and more voluptuous of the hens near him, suddenly began to cluck, thundered his wings and leapt with all the vigor of the winter sun upon her. The three younger chickens and the proprietor watched them with his beloved and the two walked quickly across the road together.

The young cock now looked at the slender hen who had begun rather furtively to resume her meal. He walked uncertainly toward her increasing his pace as he came. She pretended not to notice but in a fit of inexperience he hesitated at her side, then she had to scream and run, wings out zigzag down the road. He careened after her beating his puerile wings and shortening his stride afraid to overtake her. She ran straight to the master cock who appraised the situation instantly and without ruffling his feathers put the young whippersnapper in his place. Immediately they all resumed the business of eating.

The proprietor had watched the drama spellbound. Now he came suddenly to life, kissed and hugged his child several times, walked rapidly back and forth and then called for his servant. An old woman came out of the store. He thrust the child into her arms and bounded up the stairs into his house.

I slid to the other window of the car and looked up over the wall at the top of Lingaraj. It was remarkably beautiful thrust against the blue sky. Seeing it from here was like reading a book backwards; seeing the top first, the great fluted disk of stone, the finial and the iron trident of Shiva piercing up beyond itself.

It was irresistible. I got down from the car to look for a better viewpoint. I found a small temple nearby that we could enter, and the guides had gone from the platform area. This was better, this was seeing it with my own eyes. Here were broken stones, a precarious secret of balance, vines that clasped the stones, even a watchful snake coiled the silk cord of its body under a near tilted stone and tested the atmosphere for my intentions with its flashing tongue.

As I saw the temple reveal itself with its complex ascensions and curves, rising in quiet, carrying the sweet earth as far as possible, then speeding up in enticing curves to lead by persuasion. Here the sequence of the temples were stair-steps to revelation, from low to high, from pyramid to pyramid to summit, and on the way were proofs of triumph, dominant lions, griffins, guardians to imagination. What it would be like to stand beside it, to touch the powerful stones of its body, to look up and up to its proud crown I could only imagine. I stepped down and we went back to the car.

We drove through the town and into the countryside, passing a small temple in a shelter of trees. Further on, another stood in an open field. Then the road curved through a canopy of branches to the site of Muktesvara, still very close to Bhuvaneswar. One approaches an exquisite pink temple that has looked at the green pool at its feet for over a thousand years. This, more than any building I have seen, is a jewel, a brilliantly cut pink gem surrounded by moving dark emerald waters and trees. It is crisp, and skillfully developed, and there is a release of astonished happiness.

As I looked at the free-standing, monumental gateway I wondered if we could do a thing like this today. Not copy it – anyone with enough training can copy a work of art – but can we leap into the hidden places of consciousness and return with such treasures? If we feel inner drives of discovery can we step out of our rigid drill and stake claims in the universe as individuals? Not as puppets on wires but as freestanders who see into ourselves clearly enough to discover rare dimensions and show them to others? Tomorrow we would journey to Konarak, the Temple of the Sun.

Before we stepped from the car after the long rough drive to Konarak we were surrounded by coconut boys. They were beautiful smiling children with long curved knives and baskets of coconuts ready to be opened by a chop of the knife for drinking.

We walked away but a boy misunderstood something I had said and knocked open a coconut. He was crestfallen because of his mistake and philosophically drank the juice himself. In a moment Ben, who had not seen the episode, decided to drink a coconut and reached for it from another boy, whereupon the first in a hurry to retrieve his profits knocked open another coconut just too late. As he realized that it was a double loss his expression was so tragic that I had to buy it from him.

The sand has drifted high against Konarak, so that high on the incline you stand on the top of the outer wall and look across a broad low courtyard to the monumental Sun Temple. The photographs and drawings cannot prepare one for the power of this massive building. We had agreed that it would be worth seeing, but thought from the photos it had been overrated. Now as we stood looking at it we were aware how wrong we had been.

We hurried along the top of the wall to where large stones had been stacked as steps into the courtyard. Down them, past two massive stone elephants who stood proudly facing the temple, over broken stones and rubble, to the colossal pyramid itself. It is the assembly hall, one of the three temple elements and all that is left intact of the grandeur of the Temple of the Sun. The entire temple represented a great stone chariot, a unique and stupendous conception. It was the last and greatest achievement of the Orissan builders.

'Surya, the Sun God, flashes through the sky in a stone winged chariot yoked to seven sun horses. Ten stone wheels spin in the sand as the sun horses plunge. Forever speeds the temple toward the sea.'

This is the ancient literature, the temple itself, direct and simple to understand in variable form and infinite detail. Everything under the sun – yes, everything, in laceworks of carving that cover every inch of the building, with fragile vine tendrils or great chunks of plain stone sculpture. All vigor, all charming chiaroscuro of shadow and light, all the animate imagery of earth moving in bands of stone, up and up, in forms of increasing purity and innocence which at last dissolve into sunlight.

The sculpture is erotic in the lowest parts and especially startling to the notion that sex belongs to darkness. The scholar may be right who says that the Tantric ritual that produced this temple caused the racial stock to disappear. He justifies the theory by the fact that the men here now could not produce these temples. Perhaps the local Orissans would be unable to produce another Konarak, but I suspect that neither could the present-day Westerners produce another Chartres, and no Tantric ritual to blame.

At the west end of the temple stands a pile of stones that was once a part of the construction, the mandapa or prayer hall. This mountain of carved blocks, some broken by a fall, some lying intact as if humming with the life of the chisel, tell the story of a disaster. Before the highest monoliths were put in place the foundations began to crumble and spoil a vision that had been raised course by course, year after year on that initial miscalculation. Imagine the moment of discovery, the stunned architects, the tense whispering that rustled among the workmen, the sudden rebellion of their composite mind and the futile energies to save. Then the slow unbelieving abandonment. On the ground near the broken stones that have fallen during the centuries great figures carved for the top lie waiting for ascension, forged iron beams some almost forty feet long lie ready to be put in place as support for a massive crown of stone. The long earth ramp up which the stones were pushed to the top has blown and washed away long ago, and on the rubble of the ruins we climbed to a cornice. From the terraces formed by that ledge, we looked down into the well that had been the tower. Stairs, perhaps built into the tower during its construction, took us down. The inner shrine would have been here and the base for the idol was in place, a huge monolith of dark green chlorite ten feet square and two feet thick carved all around with a deep frieze of figures, rows of attendants to the Sun God.

A couple in matching blue jeans, plaid shirts, and long billed caps were scrambling over the temple; several families with small children strolled near us; young men appeared in clusters here and there on the pyramid top of the temple to wave and shout at their friends below. But one scarcely noticed them in the shadow of the mighty stones. The scale of the building turned them into miniatures and their shouts into murmurs in the still air.

To the south stood a remarkable sculpture. The war horses reared beside their running attendants. They were superb. A scholarly man draped with an arsenal of cameras stopped beside us.

'A masterpiece, don't you think?' he asked. We agreed and walked with him around the platform. 'This group is shown on an issue of our stamps, you may have remembered,' he continued. 'It is considered to equal the sculpture of Han China.'

He pointed to a flat roofless structure to the east of the assembly hall. 'That is the Dancing Hall. When you stand there remember that the sea which is now three miles away was then just beyond the wall.'

He left us and we walked over the the Dancing Hall. It was high, supporting rows of stone pillars on which another pyramidal roof would have rested. We looked east. Sand uninterrupted in its long course covered the rising coastal plain that seven hundred years ago was under the sea.

I sat there on a broken column in the Dancing Hall for a long time. Children ran from pillar to pillar then back down the steps to their picture-taking parents. On raised ground to the left of the temple near colossal stone elephants sat a band of pilgrim priests, young gentle-faced men who sat in rows eating their afternoon meal, in silence looking at the temple. No cameras for them. They exercised their perception, discovering themselves in what they saw.

Thank God, I thought, that no two things, or people or places or nations are alike; that there is a simple and a complex; that there is strength of strength, and strength of fragility; that there is action, and like a pool of still wine, intoxicating quiet. Thank God, for the infinite variety of earth.

10

Poetry

A week after our marriage in San Francisco in 1946 I sat in our Chinatown studio happily sorting papers that had been stuffed in suitcase pockets, old handbags and other corners during my travels. The reluctance of parting with useless friendly things, little comforting things of my premarried life led me to prolong the existence of certain lines of poetry I'd written over the years, most, I thought, not finished. Showing them to Ben on their way to the waste basket, I gave him the finished ones first. He read through them, nodded and smiled. Then apologetically I handed him the scraps. He read. He sat up. He turned slowly around with deep eyes. 'These are good. They're wonderful! They're taut and free. I've just bought a book of poems for your birthday – coals to Newcastle!'

So the book began. I wrote then – and still do – at night. A pad and pencil, no lights, feeling the edges of the page, seeing, hearing the words come spinning out of nowhere. In his sleep Ben would hear the pencil-scratch, mumble with a chuckle 'The presses are rolling tonight,' and go back to sleep.

I'd sent some to publishers. 'Your remarkable poems . . . Fresh images . . . Saxon rhythms.' But no publication (though the *Pakistan Quarterly* in Karachi had published some of my illustrated poems in 1953).Then after thirteen years of writing, a book was on the horizon.

Calcutta is a city profoundly Indian, not cosmopolitan, but where thought nevertheless is stirred by breezes from the world as by the evening wind. Calcutta was the city of the semi-invalid philosopher Abu Sayed Ayyub in whose book-lined study we have heard Indian wisdom in western words, over tea and Bengali delicacies and the reading of Indian poetry. Without explanation Ayyub read a Tagore poem in Bengali, and an ancient Sanskrit poem, then a modern Bengali poem by Buddha Dev Bose. I couldn't appreciate them of course by language, but listening, suddenly responded with a sense of coming focus. 'That last one, Ayyub. It seemed to come through even without understanding a word of it.' 'Because you're a modern, Emily. That was Buddha Dev's.' Ayyub, the editor of *Quest*, the English-language magazine, published a number of my poems, and an article by Ben. Ayyub, slender as a wand, wrapped in a cocoon of shawls to ward off chill on the hottest nights, Ayyub in starched white on the speaker's platform . . . with his little son Pushpa, beautiful as a medieval icon.

We had met several Bengali poets. One, Buddha Dev Bose, was in fact an eminent figure in Bengali and Indian-English literature. He liked the poems. The Rupa Press decided to publish with the understanding that I would select the printer and supervise every detail of publication. I was determined that the format would be my own work too, and was proud when it won the India National Best Award. After discussions and taxiings through the densest sections of Calcutta, I found my printer – a man of imagination. There was an ease of exchange, a play of expressions that said 'we're knowing this *together*' with Sailendranath Guha Ray, founder of the Sri Saraswati Press.

S. N. Guha Ray included a small chin, prominent teeth, near-sighted eyes. The small moustache and big horn-rimmed glasses were afterthoughts. There was a year of work together. Two or three times a week I slipped into one of the battery of chairs that faced him across his desk, clutching sheafs of poems, proofs, samples of stock. The print and all the array of papery stuff on his desk was aflutter in the jet-stream pounding down from a ceiling fan and just once in that sweating clangorous year I saw him pull off his glasses to wipe the perspiration from his eyes. I wouldn't have known him on the street without them. These were the eyes of the idealist that he was, of the firey young man who had asked Mahatma Gandhi how he could help the Freedom Movement. A press, the Mahatma had told him. Print the Freedom Movement, the knowledge of it, get out information, notices, rally the people. Saraswati, Goddess of Knowledge . . . Guha Ray, a few friends, a clandestine press in a basement. Then it became a mobile press moving from place to place to keep the people informed.

He put on his glasses and lo, there was the immaculately groomed, humorous, debonair Managing Editor of one of the largest and best presses in India. We liked each other, he liked my poetry. Once when he was stubborn – and business-like – I wept, tears mingling with the dripping perspiration, and won. His bearer seeing me come in would burst into grins and produce tea. The best tea in Calcutta. Guha Ray had a fancy tea-set for me; I poured. He took saccharine. I, ample sugar. We sipped tea. He attended to business, handing me a book or magazine just opened from the mail, then sent me home with his car and driver.

I decided to call the book *Poems and Epigrams* because many are short swift ideas seen with a glance of the imagination. None was about India as is my prose account of *Delhi, Old and New* published by Rand McNally 1963. However, most of them, being feelings not easily spoken, were as true for Indians as for the rest of us. They were what is called 'lyric' poetry – the kind I didn't like before I began to write it.

I wrote my Aunt Lillian Morris that I was publishing a book of poetry – although I had not heard from her for several months after Uncle Vere died. Then without reference to my book she wrote several long letters. No mention of her San Francisco shop, her daily life, nor of things of current interest. Fanciful letters, memories of her childhood, and scenes of travels: crossing the Montana plains at night, seeing the lonely lights; then the Alps and seeing a light far across the valley.

I did not tell her that the book was to be my 'thank you' for all she meant to me, keeping the small insignia in the front – the Dove family crest that she prized – as a surprise. Months, months of producing the book, the fabric of the binding a trick of reversed cloth, and end papers placed as I determined; the spine flat. I was a vixen for perfection, and as dearly as Guha Ray loved me, I knew that I was pressing for an excellence that his fellow directors questioned. The book was in labor, Guha Ray officiating and here was the first copy, sent to me by his driver.

Outside a flashing October storm beat on the leaves and windows – thunder, lightning, the monsoon's final fury before it would retreat. The book in my hand, I signed this first copy 'To

Lili from Emily', wrapped it, and as a climax of rain crashed in splendor through the garden compelling the trees to proclaim their exuberance, I wrote to my beloved Lili, 'A storm is sweeping through the garden, tossing the trees, crashing rains bring resounding accolades against my window – storms that you love; storms are your pleasant weather . . . My book to you has come just now. The first copy to tell you how everything I am or will be has been your making.' Next morning the letter and the book were sent.

In the afternoon a telegram from my brother. 'Aunt Lillian sinking fast. Can you come.' I got there on the first commercial jet flight around the world three days after she died, her death culminating a year of illness she would let no one tell me of. My letter came on her last day. She never saw or knew it.

The timings of love? So pin-pointed in their dance, their large cruelty. I still tremble with the injustice of that timing. How could the gods have refused her – and me – my atonement, those three days?

11

Farewell
1963

Puri is an ancient town on the coast of Orissa about 200 miles southwest of Calcutta. The continuous stretch of white sand beach was almost always empty to the fresh sea and the sun. We stayed on the edge of the sands, with tamarisk trees dotting the banks of a natural lotus pond where children tussled over the flowers. Lined along the shore are the tumbled-down brick and plaster beach homes of the English and of the Rajas of palmier days, utterly deserted now with sand drifts often up to window level. In the early mornings at four o'clock I would be up to see the fishermen go out to sea. Their boats were made of shaped logs, lashed with rope, two men in the small boats and six or eight in the larger. Getting these heavy craft into the surf each day was a job that needed all hands, old and young. And then as the sun began to push above the ocean the boats would be out and away, to return about ten with their catch which was divided and sold at the waters edge after the great nets were pulled in. This, with the catch from Chilka Lake nearby, is the main source of Calcutta's fish supply, a lifeline for Bengal. Occasionally we went to the evening bazaars in the old town, where caparisoned elephants loomed up in the dark, to buy the beautifully detailed Orissa paintings of the gods and goddesses. And one evening we went to an unexpected circus, Western style.

The temple at Puri is one of the finest of ancient works, still very much in use. Foreigners are forbidden entry. One climbs a library across the street and yet another lookout spot on the far side to catch glimpses over the high compound walls. And there are six other smaller temples, each of a different sort in out-of-the-way spots that take persistent searching out. The temple priests in their zealous guardianship of the holy places sometimes met us with unfriendliness. Here is India at its most fascinating – and with some of the legendary morbidities tossed in for good measure. There is of course nearby Konarak, hard to reach in the rainy season, with its magnificent sculpture, and there is Bhuvaneswar not far away with the Lingaraj Temple, one of the three or four great buildings of India.

At Puri perhaps, more than anywhere else, the lure of adventure calls back: Chilka Lake, the Juggernaut festival, a Raja's invitation unaccepted, research amid the myriad temples of old Bhuvaneswar – a lovely one almost uniquely I think, dedicated to Brahma, or Knowledge, where I heard flute melodies played by shepherd lads; and always the thought of buying an old beach bungalow, renovating a home on the shore. And when the summer wind, the fine sand, and the wet heat make the beach less comfortable the inland rice fields, lotus ponds, and the neat tribal villages would be there. The excitement of current enterprise with the enormous earth dam at Hirakud and the steel town of Rourkela where we did so much work is a part of Orissa too. And there was the office building at nearby Choudwar. But it would be mainly the sun, sand, and sea of Puri Beach that I, myself, would claim.

For some, it would be Darjeeling in the Himalayas with its astounding view of Kanchenjanga, the world's third highest mountain as it rises forty miles away from nearly sea-level in the precipitous Ranjit gorge to a final 28,140 feet. Its gigantic serenity, seen from top to bottom, dwarfs the American Rockies and makes the beauties of Switzerland seem an incident. The scale of the very foothills is beyond description as they move towards the great snow wave that is crowned by Kanchenjanga. One may rise early to drive in a jeep up Tiger Hill to view Mount Everest, and, sure enough, Everest can be seen, a white dot in the vast mountain landscape. But it is Kanchenjanga that awes one to silence, as it takes its orange form in the sunrise beyond the fresh green of a few close pine boughs.

Well, we shall claim both of these, each with space to grow.

There comes a day when it is right to return for a time to one's native land. For us it was in late 1963: the excitement and sadness of seeing an America not so young. And we, immersed in ever new-old ideas of continuity, found a starker light to live by than the singing in our hearts would have wished.

How the great monsoon pours rain through the Bengal green and the hot fresh smells of earth reach back . . .

Postlude

In 1958 while considering a Western architectural competition, I developed some thoughts for new support methods for very large buildings which have since found their way into the architectural press, but they illustrate the quandary of this century as its technological potential emerges. This is not the place for detail. Suffice it to say that the building itself is a special type of hydraulic jack which eliminates the normal compression in vertical members, and this in turn minimizes the amount of structural material needed, thus making possible, theoretically, the construction of exceedingly high structures. But *why* so high? Probably that question is not for architects, but again, for history to answer. The spectacular *dis*advantage of very high density living which new structural and power developments may make technically possible would reflect a society to which I would say 'no'!

In humanity's confrontation with the issues of the future America is on the firing line. Its vast wealth – the result of the amazing material success of our political, economic, agricultural, and industrial systems – thrusts it head-on into technology. America is face-to-face with questions not yet in sight for most of the rest of the world. The United States is again the frontier.

What will we make of our place in history? If it is to be a place worthy of the pioneers who once made their brave and simple march across the continent, there is but one option: the option of self-restraint. This journey, when we have courage to set out, will be far different from the pioneers', but it will need the same qualities in our people: hard-headed knowledge, self-surrender, faith, and self-discipline – they will all be necessary – all. The price of democracy is self-control. Perhaps America will not pay that price, or have the courage to defend these qualities.

Negativism, self-indulgence, and self-doubt are paths to disintegration.

Not used to the habit-forming narcotic of push-button 'entertainment' and the unrelieved mechanical noise that had captured our countrymen in the '50s we looked on America of the 1960s in bewilderment. The barrage of unnecessary 'comforts', the mind-programming techniques of the psychoanalysts, the substitute for personal action in the truly wicked impact of television – had changed America. We saw that resplendent world shackled with luxuries. We heard the voice of the 'new morality' – which is no morality, but a subtle network of ignorance, hypocrisy, perversion, and boredom. We found normal, healthful motives reduced to qualities called, euphemistically, enlightened tolerance, behaviorism, relativism, and permissiveness – all of which can turn children and then humanity itself back to the jellyfish of primordial ooze. We heard a peculiar vocabulary: 'image', 'stance', 'dialogue', 'meaningful' – all words that are veils between ourselves and reality – hypnotic shields between fact and conscience. The amazing skill in manipulating untruths was called sophistication, a vicious game of make-believe made fashionable and glib by the ultimate lie: the medium is the message.

The sign of these extraordinary changes? – changes that seemed incoherent, unrelated, until we understood the one new ingredient that had come to our America while we were away, the small coffin in every home, the black box rigged with its lethal powers of persuasion, fronted by its dead eye that with a touch of the button leaps to simulated vision and sees for us so that we do not need to see for ourselves – the 'communications' media that is so skilfully designed not to communicate – the ultimate weapon which we use upon ourselves. How can it matter if the programs are 'good' or 'bad'? For young people passivity itself is the killer. And faith? How does faith mature in young minds when the shock for 'now' is fed each day on television? How is born a new esthetic for new technologies, or how is discovered the spirit of the place if first intuitions are obliterated, or programmed to fit the mass; when children's fore-reachings are inhibited by fake 'solutions'; when rock music leads on to dope?

Is there perhaps still time in America and in the West when

absolute, not relative, values can be correlated and focused on action; when the persuit of happiness is seen to mean fulfilment of gifts – a better skier, a better scholar?

Commitments like these could be, as Karl Barth, the great Christian theologian, has said, 'fruit that grows . . . upon the tree of history between God and man', for we must stand upon that history, upon that human geometry. Freedom and obligation are a package deal. It is impossible to visualize another world. Though so different from America, our India in its first years of promise reinforced this knowledge – for it is true the world around.

Appendix

REPRODUCED FROM BENJAMIN POLK'S
ARCHITECTURE AND THE SPIRIT OF THE PLACE
PUBLISHED CALCUTTA 1961

Appendix

It is necessary to consider how town planning also, as an extension of Architecture, derives its strength and colour from these deep connections to what we see and feel about us.

Town planning is not office work, is not the drawing board thinking that today forms an ineffective substitute for the vital planning process, a process that was the very climax of human expression in the days of the cathedral and the temple builders. For it was planning when civic leaders of the site, addressing themselves to its visual and functional merits, decided to place a major building just here and not there. It was planning indeed when farmers gathered their dwellings together on a rise for protection against marauders or perhaps to conserve rich low-lying lands for crops. And it was planning of some consequence when the Greeks sited the Parthenon with its dramatically subtle angle of approach on the Acropolis. One knows that none of this siting was done with pencil and paper. It is only from the peak of the Eiffel Tower that we can discover the full effect of drawing board plans. But our world remains an eye-level world and the neighbourhood is still to be walked in.

The measure of our skill in dealing with this world is found in many small ways—making a path or building a house. Look for example at the natural vegetation and its trees. Are the trees brought into our hearts by their new relationship to our man-made work? Does the scale of our design reinforce the scale of nature so that our work overflows the bounds of mere brick and mortar to include the very lie of the land? If so, our work has been reverently conceived and lovingly executed, and the natural world of our site is itself more beautiful than before ; if not, we have failed in our profession and our art. Love for the land gives the intuition of artistry, and the sharing with others of these perceptions may be the beginning of true Tradition in its fine and proper sense.   Understanding what we see, our resources are renewed and we in turn may bring this renewal to the land. The wheel moves round and something of beauty enters our undertakings.   The Architect as a growing point of the community, is part and parcel of its strengths—perhaps also of its weaknesses.   But aware of the genius of the place, he conserves and amplifies, if he is worthy of his hire, the essential beauty of his site knowing that each person and each place has special significance, that each is a special case.

In the countryside we learn from nature more quickly than in cities but today we can merge the experience of town and country, so that whether deep in a metropolis or out in the fields there can be a satisfying balance.   To planning of towns we can bring the experience of seasonal rhythms, letting the countryside enter small-scale elements of the city's structure.   It is within these elements that intimate personal relationships of small groups play a critical role.   These groups will establish themselves as communities of close neighbours.   Their locales will be distinguished visually from other locales.   In the country the functional limits of village, field, and forest tend to be naturally determined by the lie of the land.   In the city, dwellings must be grouped to form tiny neighbourhoods within which are spaces developed in convexities and concavities forming the texture of the plan. In these relationships, both tangible and intangible, is to be found the frontier where the frame-work of local community can begin to seize the initiative away from paralysing centralism.   Here locales and groups, buildings and men, are the stuff of Architecture and planning.

'The sense of scale is the most important tool of a town planner. One can refer to photography or drawings, or better yet walk through a variety of Indian cities both beautiful and ugly: say Jaipur and some of the larger villages in the Punjab, the temple cities of Saurashtra, or one can discover the quality of Banaras, and the old spacious sections of Port Cochin in the South, seeing now each of these reflects the judgement of its time and place, and now each illustrates fine man-made geography.   One could analyse the largest angle of vision which gives an instantaneous impact to the eye, and find that in the vertical direction two-thirds of this angle is about 30 degrees above eye-level.   One would determine the fact that a human face is not clearly and quickly recognized at a distance of much more than 80 or 90 feet, and one would experiment with greater distances and discover that no object can be seen at all at a greater distance than 3,500 times its size. Also one would experience the reasoning behind the fact that the best ratio between the two dimensions of a plaza should not exceed one is to three. One could gradually and by experiment sense what is the intimate human scale for a neighbourhood of homes with the perennial sense of surprise and discovery in these heart-warming cities of India. One would enjoy the spirit of the place of each of them, so different one from another—yet each inevitably arousing the conviction of rightness, of fitness, and of complete suitability for its time and place.'*

The optimum sizes of particular cities are today very much in question—most being too large for efficiency or ease of living. But in all cities we need to bring the productive side of rural areas into the pattern of the city so that townsman and countryman are less differentiated and less specialised than at present. Mutual interest between town and country in practical ways, expressed ultimately in terms of land use, landscape, and buildings will lead us away from the isolation from which both ways of life suffer. In parts of the U.S.A., for example northern Ohio, this merging is noticeable already. In recent decades the population movements out of the city to the suburbs have expressed, although often in an undesirable form, the personal needs of the denizens of the megalopolis. This effort to have the best of both worlds points up the urgency that planners be inspired designers who can give to the changing visual and social scene its realization and its form.

Britain's Sir Charles Reilly has indicated the advantages of a small group of dwellings centered on a precinct. Again, the 'green wedge', consisting of open country leading straight into a city, is a transition area which can be further refined, like the American superblock, into networks of local greenery with appropriate loggias or planted windbreaks for rest, reflection, games and outdoor work, each related to the other by footpath only. Always and ever, walking is the natural mode of progression. At

* From the author's talk on the National Programme, All India Radio on Architecture and Town Planning, Oct., 1960.

this pace we can absorb what we see and can sense the scale of our work and play. A stroll in Venice is a delight.

It was the introduction of fast wheeled vehicles, that began to disintegrate the medieval town plan. Today the necessary provision of highways will be a liability unless we reduce the need to travel. Mobility carried to its logical conclusion destroys the town. But when the problem is rightly solved multi-storey structures and free-standing one-storey homes, as well as two and three storey dwellings, will find themselves on friendly terms within one vista. The relations of these buildings and the intervening spaces they create demand our closest attention: emotional content is inseparable from functional necessity and structural logic. Reason and emotion reinforce each other, while dignity and gaiety, crispness and delicacy entwine themselves on every abstract argument and are the best conclusion of the work.

For the first time in history, men's eyes and ears are so dulled by the chaos of cities and the growing ugliness of adjacent countrysides that it seems to be difficult for the visual offenses that are peculiar to this time to be recognized. But certain insults to the human spirit are obvious: advertising bill-boards, the intrusion of automobiles, radios, and loud-speakers into every quiet space of life, repetition in the suburbs of minute mansions, the monotony of most of our public housing. These things, throughout the world, go to make up the characteristic modern landscape. A low point of history has been reached, for there is little now of that fitness of space and form which demonstrates the harmony of a culture. Unconsciously we defend ourselves against injury by learning not to see. Our sensitivity dies from lack of use—or is never born—while the concern for form and space is replaced by the word 'esthetics'.

The negative side of this, the limiting of personality by poor environment, has been analysed—even dissected—in recent years: but positive liberation through environmental dignity is beyond the ken of mere statistical planning.

II

Suitable town planning survey techniques have been developed and described by Gaston Bardet in the Town Planning Review of October 1951. His article entitled "Social Topography" points out that 'An examination of the social topography leads one to reduce the widths of certain (land use) zones to narrow strips behind the frontages, and some special frontages may be designated within zones. A zoning map should not be a harlequin's coat but rather a complex of surfaces and lines to which will be added focal points where local groups meet'. Bardet has evolved a survey notation where *each* person is represented, as the case may be, in production, commerce, residence, or agriculture. The resulting maps are complex but easily understood. He says: 'I believe that the introduction of the methods of social topography can be compared to the introduction of the microscope in biology'. 'Echelons' range from a small hamlet of five or ten families up to the neighbourhood of 500 to 1500 families. In analysing and synthesizing larger neighbourhoods or 'quarters' he has evolved the 'sociological profile' which gives, visually, the economic base of the town. Thus, an appropriate technique is available to planners who have become aware of the sterile results of the prevalent misguided sociology. Bardet concludes: 'It will be easier and safer, and results will be of longer duration, if we seek to cure our towns of the serious diseases from which they suffer by the use of micro-groups and micro-organisms instead of by vast blind plans that must be constantly revised'.

Man selects from the available sites of a region an immediate locale for his life and his work. The nature of the precise locale depends, within these limits, on the social values and the needs of the time. In a given region different localities will have been selected from age to age, according to the values of the inhabitants. Today then, although our new frontier in town planning is, to a degree, a macrocosmic one, it is, within the macrocosm, concentratedly and emphatically micro-cosmic. The specific place, the local group and its special persons are the very ground of planning, as of Architecture.

We must, especially in industrialised countries, rework our surroundings to a humane proportion, placing within easy walking distance most centers of daily affairs for each member of the family. Patrick Geddes used the term 'conservative surgery' to denote perceptive readjustments of the local scene designed to achieve these ends. Readjustment, and not rebuilding, will usually be the only economical mode of approach to urban redevelopment. It is significant that Geddes worked out and applied this idea to Indian cities during his long stay in this country, and it remains still the realistic mode of approach everywhere, since drawings on paper, made as if we had somehow taken a fresh start, can seldom be applied in practice.

The notion that industry must be set apart in zones well separated from zones of residence, as if each activity of life were antagonistic with the other, shows an unbalanced analysis of man's nature. We must take industrial activities, except noxious ones or noise makers, into our landscapes, bringing homes to them ; for it is quite impossible to understand and love ones home locale if the journey to work divides our life and makes our work a different thing from living. Industry needs 'green factories'.

The amplification of what we may call the transition zone, the zone of interplay between different types of land use, whether farmland, neighbourhoods of homes, or in the larger sphere of the region, eliminates both visual monotony and crude contrast. The modulation of a skillfully wrought landscape reflects the continuous subtleties of this 'edge condition'. In animal distribution in the wilds, physical barriers and microclimates and local topography, more closely define the species habitats than do generalized areas. Likewise in human affairs there is drama where two concepts meet, and the transition between them is conducive to the surprises that bring vitality to the landscape. These transitions often consist of areas of multiple use and they determine the quality of the landscape.

Geometrically, a smaller area has a very much greater proportion of 'edge' than a large area, and since edge conditions are vital ones this reinforces the necessity for detailed, intimate designs. This is true geometry for town planning. Communication routes may naturally become a function of the edge and waterways for instance, are potentially the finest parks. Motorways linked with footways and properly planted with native trees can likewise serve the principle of multiple use.

'For the large city, the garden neighbourhood will have to be combined with planned neighbourhoods of much higher densities, planned for some who will wish to live in high free-standing towers, some in side-by-side dwellings surrounding small squares and parks, and yet some who will want the exciting chaos of the bohemian parts of a London or a New York. This variety is a legitimate demand upon the planner and it is usually his weakest point. Neighbourhoods of mixed dwelling types are very much in order.'*

We must have small parks close to the family, for these small open spaces are the key to satisfying city life. As the natural world enters these spaces we may perhaps discover the fitting adaptation of each site to its purpose, just as Japanese gardens demonstrate in their own way this process of adaptation. The resort to aggressive control of ones materials, whether it be in land management or zoning, does violence to the values of our new frontier where there is never any average-best-pattern ; where we are always developing the special case.

In a study called Man For Himself: An Inquiry into the Psychology of Ethics, Eric Fromm writes, 'our moral problem . . . lies in the fact that we have lost the sense of the significance and the uniqueness of the individual, that we have made ourselves into instruments for purposes outside ourselves, that we experience and treat ourselves as commodities, and that our own powers have become alienated from ourselves. "Realists" are ignorant of some hard facts. They do not see that the emptiness and planlessness of individual life, that the lack of productiveness and the consequent lack of faith in oneself and in mankind, if prolonged, result in emotional and mental disturbances which would incapacitate man even for the achievement of his material aims.

The experience of 'relation' may ultimately reconstitute our knowledge and save us from these depths. The equal importance of means with ends is the first frame of reference. The acquisition of leisure after an eight hour day of meaningless routine—whether it be on the production line or as an executive —does not give the hoped-for happiness. Mass production has brought also mass entertainments, spectator sports, and the multiplication of trivialities mis-called the higher standard of living. Neither physically nor spiritually can the human frame long withstand this onslaught. But mechanical ingenuity can on the other hand be devoted to evolving machine methods for creative work, methods which would merge work with leisure ; for the proper test of planning is that each person may find his own best

* ibid.

functions, and voluntarily choose to integrate them with his fellows.

Our civilization is not a scientific one ; it is technological, the result of applied science only, mass produced and mass designed ; and the mass can manifest itself only in slavery. It may submit to Communism or to Fascism ; or to some other form of bureau-cracy. More often tyranny is a combination of all these. Technology has had a large part to play in this development of mass-mindedness. Here, the Architectural counterpart of the matter is seen in a smokescreen of refined techniques where the creation of inspired space is a memory of the past (the word 'monumental' is already in disuse) and where all is a facade to hide gadgetry, surface without form ; while designers, taking seriously the restless tricks of world fairs, lead us farther down the des-perate path of uniformity.

The author in a previous article has written : 'The essence of Architecture is the design (or discovery) of space in such a way that human sensibilities are heightened. Let us stay close to this thought. For the past ten thousand years man has not changed biologically as far as is known, and his inherent sense of the fitness of things, the satisfaction of his inborn demands his capacity for inspiration through his own self-created environment, are evi-dently basic to his nature, almost constant facts ; and the distinc-tive spatial concepts that comprise architectural history have not violated man's ten thousand year old nature. The rich variety of the world is proclaimed by differing cultures, expressing them-selves through architectural forms, flowers on a tree nourished by the earth from which it springs. Their logic rises superior to reasonings, and their validity is the validity of personality. Variety, therefore, is inevitable. . . . But the raking up of (historical) stylistic mannerisms and their application to the fronts and tops of reinforced concrete frames is not of course architec-ture in any case'.*

III

We return again and again to our well-spring. The under-standing of natural relationships points to our own role in the world. The earth's vegetation makes a place for us, feeding and

* Marg, June 1956.

sheltering our lives, and it inexorably tends towards a necessary equilibrium with climate, soil and animal life. This is the characteristic of organic growth. The succession of changes presented by a landscape over a period of time is the natural planning called ecology, and the fact that every landscape when undisturbed arrives at a balance that expresses its best potential leads us to see our role in discovery, rather than in conquest. As with the management of land where the existing community of vegetation indicates the past and future of the area, so in human ecology and human geography it is possible to predict the future, expressing this prediction in great Architecture and wise planning.

When led by art and governed by religion, the environmental sciences, read stereoscopically with human geography, will reveal our general and particular relation to the universe, and will aim at understanding the profound effect of nature—and of man himself—upon mankind ; and they will show the earth and the solar system to be the sympathetic field of our existence. (See the magnificent first developments in solar heating, solar power, and power from wind and tides.) The large geographical region, often unrelated to national boundaries—for nationalism is itself an outdated concept—can be the half-way house between the small locality and the affairs of one world. Integration and co-ordination are still the principal jobs for Regional planners—but in a new context. Leaving aside the success or failure of wide-spread birth control measures, the world's population will in any case rise from 2700 million in 1958 to 4000 million in 1980. Without successful control it will rise to 7000 million in the year 2000. Whether we wish it or not, vast changes will be required which will enormously intensify rural land use throughout the world. A multi-purpose regional pattern will be forced upon us, with the implications for Architecture and town planning noted above. The argument is again reinforced by considerations beyond our control.

We must pick our way among the profitless boulders of professional double-talk to the rich lode of a 'return'. But once sensing what is given us to do we soar in flight, building, perhaps, prophetically. We are spoken to and we reply, giving life to limitations that lovingly transcend us : limits that wish to be born again by laws of liberty, growing as our spirit grows. We live out the paradoxical union of freedom and necessity. We are not able to compromise with a work seeking to be born. We are alone with it. All that happens is manifest and self-evident.

He who is aware of his time, fully aware of this 20th century, knows certainly that neither the state, nor any mere institution, can yield either the life-giving relations of community or the inspiration of art. Community, if we found it, would depend upon a living source just as also the effective action that flows from our relationship with that source constitutes our art. To live in this dependence is to know freedom. This boundary is fulfilment.

It needs a clearing of rank weeds to get at the roots of form and function today, to come to grips with Architecture. Mass production of catch-phrases is done at the risk of democracy itself and now we have cash-on-hand and but little invested capital ; so many easy words, but much less vital effort. The latest gadget is palatable, and the machine for comfort replaces the dignity of space humanly conceived. Architecture is many things, but its greatness is first, last, and always in the quality of interior and exterior space, and we lose our confidence and become less than men if we sell it over to the box-makers, the gadget vendors, the inventors, and the decorators. Before we build we need to disentangle easy words from the firm three dimensional realities of volume, mass, scale, line, proportion, ornament, colour and texture as these inhere in structural form set to the service of men ; for these realities remain paramount and permanent.

Farther back in time and deeper in need lies the very genesis of building. We require a protected place to sleep, for safety, perhaps also for comfort, during our helpless hours of unconsciousness. But these requirements are set over and over again in a different time and place—each unique, never precisely the same.

Every part of the world and every place in which we build is governed by two great prime movers: the energy of the sun and the earth's orderly force of gravity. The sun's seasons give change to architecture and the earth's gravity gives stability: the window, the pinnacle ; or the foundation and base. In the north, with less of the life-giving sun, men have wished to be known by the window and the pinnacle. In the south, shamed by the all encompassing energy of solar power, we have wished to be known by the foundation and the base. Everywhere gravity is the wise determinant of the structure. The cube of the linear dimension gave us weight, and this settled once and for all both the absolute size of the human figure and the scale of man-made landscape. Sometimes with eager perception and sometimes with reluctance, but always perforce with obedience, we have wrought with the wise force of the earth and the sharp force of the sun. In some places—France, India, China, the organic solidarity of human geography is old ; elsewhere it may be new. Age hallows the ground of our work. Youth gives it keenness. The building, the landscape, the region, all together are the physical expression of our life, and when life grows sensitively in its environment its expressions will differentiate themselves and its vitality will produce rich textures and joyful variations. Fine buildings are climaxes of geography. They become possible when the Architect has brought his science and his technique to terms with the rootedness of his spirit ; when he feels the sweep of history and knows the seasons' changes, and when he finds himself at one with the purposes and customs of his people. Then as he rejoices in the significant and the particular of his immediate programme, he will submerge and depersonalize himself in his work, and will know the thrill of the divination of forms. He will hold mysterious converse with the tutelary genius of the Place. And through this converse his art will receive strong imprints from the natural world and its human counterpart. We have called this the frame of the encounter ; a voyage of discovery ; a growing point ; or a fulfilment. This, and nothing less than this, is the necessary history of Architecture. Today's self-consciousness must fall away as we seize space for our lives ; and as our driving forces integrate with our interpretations of history we must come to know where we stand, or we will be swept along with foolish fashions, being reasonable at each stage of our retreat. If we are to preserve temper and focus in our hearts and minds we will need an inward and an outward vision, and above all we will need aid from the conserving power of the natural world, and refreshment from the corroborating evidence of harmony with it.

Architecture is the visible link between the spiritual and material parallels of our lives. It is a flux of subject and object. Our landscapes witness the quality and tendency of our living, and in turn our living in good measure is determined by our man-made landscape. Recall the decline of North Africa after the departure of the Romans whose remarkable irrigation works were abandoned by the Vandals and nomadic Arabs. Goats took over the ploughed fields. Deforestation rapidly followed. Today we have deserts where there was formerly a partnership between man and nature. Man-made landscape has indeed determined North African life. Parallel dynamics are found in Architecture: the great city for example. He who would build in New York today does his work in a wholly man-made world. 'But the fact of the neighbourhood (whether planned for or not), the principles of human scale in civic design (ignored or not), the psychology of the small group which gives a visible characteristic setting to our self-expression (acknowledged or not), are ever-present. The unalterable axioms of human geography and human geometry encompass us even when denied. These axioms are the tangible links between our spirit and our body, and we break them at our peril. Will we be wiser than the nomads and avoid a similar fate?

Yet when all the limits are defined, there may be some who will still hold that Architecture especially now, stems from our freedom from limits, from our own conscious will. They will point to transportable structures that bear no relation to the 'spirit of the place', not seeing that these transient conveniences partake, like the glass-encased skyscrapers, more of the quality of clothes than of Architecture. And there are factories where the mechanical equipment becomes the determinant of the design. But both these considerations call us even more emphatically to the fine adjustment of the new structural techniques with the human spirit and with the Spirit of the Place, and to conceptions based on these three. Neither physical man nor geography will change. We must know ourselves and order our affairs accordingly, since machinery and its economics are our servants, not our masters.

By cohesion between land and people, buildings do in fact *become* the place, as notations of the human spirit. And thus it is not only man's life that we recognise here: it is reverence for the earth—for Place—as well. For the earth is the ground of our life. And so although the human spirit is not confinable by physical limits, it is free only to make a compact of fruitfulness with the natural world ; or it is free to destroy itself altogether, either quickly now or slowly as in former centuries. When we consider Architecture in the natural world it is found to be greatly conservative and sensitively attached and adapted to the place of its growth. When, however, Architecture is considered as the result of free will and choice it is discovered to be also prophecy. Both are true. We are most certainly fashioning our own world, succeeding as we accept gracefully the world that is given to us. But we are not in a vacuum alone with our scientists. It is not a question of what remarkable thing we are next able to do. The question we are concerned with, whether we like it or not, is the more profound and more searching question: what do we wish to *be?* What are our values? and do we recognise them in the friendly limits of our span?

From ancient China, a book on Man's freedom in his natural environment, the Tao Te Ching, has this to say:

"The men who set out to capture all under heaven and make it their own, according to my observation do not succeed.

> What is under heaven is a sacred vessel,
> Not to be treated in such fashion,
> And those who do so bring it to ruin.
> Those who hold on to it, lose it . . .
> The Way of Heaven is not to contend
>   and yet to be able to conquer,
> Not to declare its will and yet to get a
>   response,
> Not to summon but have things come
>   spontaneously,
> To work very slowly with well-laid plans.
> Heaven's net is vast with wide meshes;
> Yet nothing is lost."

Karachi Polytechnic Institute

Industrial shops, Karachi Polytechnic Institute

Tripitaka Library, Rangoon

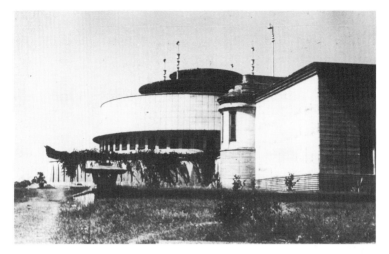

Tripitaka Library, Rangoon – exterior

Tripitaka Library, Rangoon

Jallianwalabagh National Memorial, Amritsar

Author with Prime Minister Nehru at the Jallianwalabagh

Temple of the Sun, Konarak, Orissa

Jallianwalabagh National Memorial, Amritsar

Kandariya Mahadeo Temple, Khajuraho

Temple in Bharatpur, Nepal

A street in Kathmandu

The Royal Palace, Kathmandu; marriage ceremonies

The Royal Palace, Kathmandu

Grand staircase of the Palace – wedding of the Prince Birendra,
23 February 1970

Polytechnic Institute, Sanno Thimi, Kathmandu

Polytechnic Institute, Sanno Thimi

Residence for Mr and Mrs Bharat Ram, New Delhi – from the west

From the garden (east)

Woodlands apartments, Calcutta

Minto Park, Calcutta

Aftab Gardens apartments, Calcutta

Times of India, New Delhi – press and offices

U.S. State Department staff apartments, Rangoon

Office for Tata Oil Mills, near Calcutta

Residence for Imperial Chemical Industries Ltd, Calcutta

Uktal University Library, Bhuvaneswar, Orissa

Kala Mandir Theatre, Calcutta

House, Pilani University, Rajasthan

Workmen's homes for Gwalior Rayon Ltd, Mavoor, Calicut, Kerala

Elementary school, Kirtipur, Kathmandu

Author at SCI Work Camp, near Calcutta, 1960

Emily Polk, with dragon mosaic

Above and opposite: paper print mosaics by Emily Polk

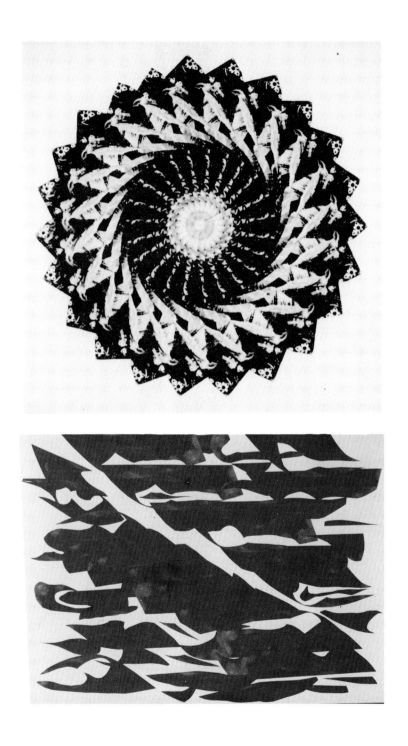

On the Hooghly: *ink painting by Emily Polk*

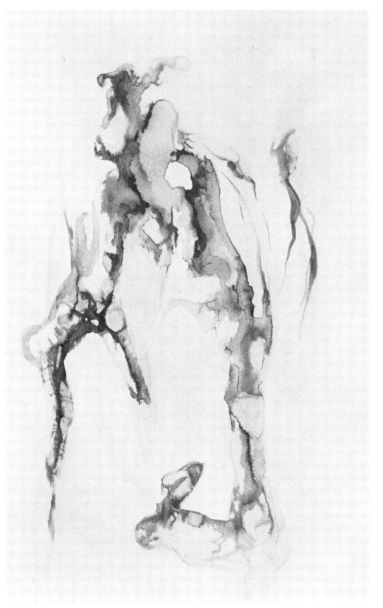

Ink painting by Emily Polk

Ink painting by Emily Polk

Wrap to be worn with saree, designed by Emily Polk
Brown and pale blues

Black and white fine wool

Cream fine wool and dark beige silk

White and light red fine wool

Mosaic print by Emily Polk: Volée

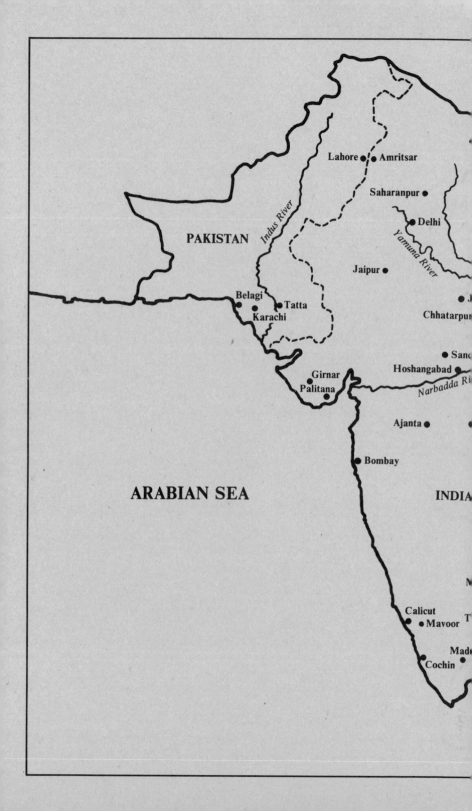